Smack, Crack and the Long Road Back

Smack, Crack and the Long Road Back

By

Phil Grimes

Copyright

Copyright © 2017 Phil Grimes

The moral rights of the author have been asserted.

All rights reserved. Apart from any fair dealing for the purposes of research or private study, or criticism or review, as permitted under the Copyright, Designs and Patents Act 1988, this publication may only be reproduced, stored or transmitted, in any form or by any means, with the prior permission in writing of the copyright owner, or in the case of the reprographic reproduction in accordance with the terms of licenses issued by the Copyright Licensing Agency. Enquiries concerning reproduction outside those terms should be sent to the publisher.

ISBN-13: 978-1999869007 (Grimes Publishing)

ISBN-10: 1999869001

Editing, formatting, and cover design by Oxford Literary Consultancy: www.oxfordwriters.com

Contents

Acknowledgements and Gratitude vii
Chapter One 1
Chapter Two 19
Chapter Three 33
Chapter Four 47
Chapter Five 63
Chapter Six 69
Chapter Seven 81
Chapter Eight 87
Chapter Nine 97
Chapter Ten 103
Chapter Eleven 111
Chapter Twelve 123
Chapter Thirteen 131
Chapter Fourteen 143
Chapter Fifteen 159
Chapter Sixteen 169
Chapter Seventeen 177
Chapter Eighteen 181
Chapter Nineteen 187
The Journey Back 199

Acknowledgements and Gratitude

To my mum and to my dad, God rest his soul, who never gave up and always believed in me.

To my children and grandchildren — without their humour and encouragement, my life would be empty.

To Alex Wade, for his legal advice and input which has been invaluable.

To Stephanie Hale and her team for bringing this book into life; Stephanie's expertise and professionalism has been second to none, brilliant.

To my colleagues at Ocean Recovery who work tirelessly in supporting and turning the lives around of those still addicted to drugs and alcohol. You are a great bunch.

To my wife, Susy, you are a massive inspiration, and your unwavering love, devotion, and patience have enriched my life.

All my teachers in life, anyone who has influenced me for the good.

Thank you.

Phil.

Chapter One

The Wrong Shade of Blue

June 1991

It was going to be another scorching hot day in hell. I watched the sun rise through my window as I lay on my bed, wide-eyed and soaked in sweat, fear tainting my perspective as I looked across to see the walls of my flat take on a life of their own. They were now breathing. As I breathed in, so did they, and then out. They advanced towards me as if they would swallow me whole. This was freaking me out. I knew this fear and had tasted it many times before. I had been throwing up for what seemed like days and had that horrible gut feeling that things had to get worse before they could get better, invading my consciousness. Shaking and shivering, my body was weak from withdrawals: heroin and methadone were not known for their mercy, but rather their harsh punishment. I huddled in the foetal position on my bed, empty and spent. It had been five days since I'd slept, and everything in my vision was hazy, and I remember thinking life wasn't such a good idea after all. Ice now ran through my bones, and my kneecaps ached like someone had taken a Black and Decker drill to them. The slow tick-tock of the wall clock reminded me that time wasn't a luxury I could afford.

My flat was a dark, tiny, and claustrophobically small box. I hated it, but at least it was a roof over my head. It was damp and cold with grease on the walls from cooking with little ventilation and stunk like a shithole. The place was kind of a statement to show just how far my standards had slipped. I wondered if this was going to be any different than my previous ten attempts to get clean; I knew it as I lay there, and the absurdity of it hit me like a ton of bricks. They had all ended in failure, every one. Now at thirty, I was asking myself some searching questions about my life. I'd spent most of my teenage and adult life in one chemical state or another; there had to be more to life than this. I now thought to myself: *Is it even possible to actually break free, spin this right around and do a total 360 degrees and get out; get rid of this chemical ball and chain and have a real life*? I had always wanted to look at the world through eyes that were focused, not blurred or pinned. How could I get my hands on some real freedom so I could at least breathe again?

What I'd once scornfully laughed away now looked like some distant heaven to me. Was I destined to be a few lines in an obituary column if I carried on? Found dead in a dirty squat with a needle in my arm? A few lines in the local paper described as one of life's losers? I could almost hear the coroner's words at my inquest, "Mr. Grimes died of drug abuse! Yet another statistic!"

At this point, I had been married to a woman who had also been a heroin addict and was now clean. Ann was tall with long dark hair and brown eyes, a woman with a lively personality. She was the type of person who was a sucker for a lost cause; she was a nice person with a big heart but saw herself as a knight in shining armour. Now I was her next project. We had met at a friend's place, where she had been living for a long time. I had gone around to have a hit with my mate and to get stoned, and she was there. I found her very friendly and talkative, and although nothing happened that evening between us, we got on well. We did not meet each other again after that night until a couple of years later in a church I had been invited to (ironically by a pharmacist who dispensed my prescription daily). The whole idea of God seemed too much like a mental health disaster to me. The whole idea of putting trust in someone you couldn't see baffled my head as I didn't trust the people right in front of me. It was from that meeting again at church that we started to see one another, and our relationship began.

Before we got married, I was in bad shape psychologically and emotionally, and generally screwed up. I wasn't feeling happy and excited like most grooms do with a future to look forward to. I felt depressed and unhappy, really quite vulnerable. Not to mention that years on the drug scene aren't the best training ground for marriage, commitment, and love. I walked down the aisle having consumed vast amounts of drugs, then finished it all off with a half bottle of vodka. Need I add that I staggered my way down the aisle? The rest was a haze.

A few weeks had gone by now, and I'd given Ann some money to keep to one side so that I could get it back from her if I wasn't able to cope with this rattle. The money was my plan B; if things went pear-shaped, I could get it off her and score some gear in a short space of time should I need to.

It was later the same day when I finally asked her. I was still sweating and shaking and had shooting pains in my legs. I had to sit down. I lowered myself awkwardly onto a fishing basket; I even said 'please' and placed my hand on her arm as she passed me. I'd always been proud of never having to beg anyone for anything, but this was different. This was not well received. I saw her face change from confusion to anger then rage in a matter of seconds. I don't remember much more than that, just shouting, screaming, and the crunching of bone, as she ran full on at me with her Doc Martens on. She booted me in the face, right on my nose. I fell backwards and did a very ungraceful backflip and landed by the kitchen sink. As I stood up, the room was spinning fast. I was trembling with anger. I wiped my nose and saw blood all over my hand. I thought, *I've got to get out of this place before I flip out.* I grabbed a bread knife from the kitchen sink. "Fuck this for a game of soldiers," I said. If I were going to go out, I'd go with a bang. I'd often said that to myself in my worst hours, and the other part of my mind would reply, "May as well be hung for a sheep as a lamb." As I staggered out of the flat, I said to myself, "This married life crack is not what I'd thought it would be; I'll never have to look at you or listen to you moaning ever again, so fuck off," and I meant it with every cell in my body.

On my way down the road, I passed a phone box, and maybe it was finally some higher sense kicking in, maybe just fear, but I stopped and called my doctor's surgery to ask the receptionist if I could see the doctor; surely my doctor would help? She said he was busy and would call back, but her voice somehow didn't sound very genuine, and I noted that certain satisfaction in her tone as my request was refused. I said I was going to do something crazy if no one could do anything to help me, but my plea fell on deaf ears. I then called the local drug team and said the same thing to them, but to no avail; they had their own live drama going on. Where was all this so-called support they so often banged on about? When I put the phone down, I was at the lowest point I think I'd ever been in my life. I thought, *Right, if that's how it is, just do it.* I jumped in a taxi and headed for the nearest chemist. It was near the community drug team's clinic, so I knew it was rammed with a wide range of Class A's.

When I arrived there, I asked the taxi driver to pull further down the street. Standing outside soaked with sweat, with my heart pounding, my hands shaking, all my senses heightened, I had passed the point of no return, and it would all be over soon. As the last customer left the chemist's counter, I walked in coolly and pretended to look at a pair of sunglasses at the counter's front.

I became uncomfortably aware of the track marks and abscesses that covered my arms in between my tattoos. Paranoia dominated my every thought. It was like everybody who looked at me penetrated my soul with their X-ray vision; they saw the real me, and if others could see the real me, then they would share my disgust and self-hatred.

I bent down and pulled the knife out of my sock, running around the gap in the counter into the pharmacy. I shouted at everyone in the store, "Stand fucking still and shut up!" This got their attention.

The pharmacist was just putting something back in a cupboard, so I walked over to him and put my knife to his throat. "Open the DDA box, and empty it into this," I said and shoved a cardboard box into his hands. He froze, and I could feel the resistance of his neck skin against my blade. I hoped and prayed that he didn't have a surge of heroism because the truth was I didn't want to be put to the test in such desperation. I wondered how messy it would be if his crisp white coat had blood around the collar. "The DDA box," I repeated. I'd suddenly become calm and composed. I shouted, "Do it NOW!" into his ear. He moved without question and rapidly filled up the cardboard box. I remember looking around at the rows of shelves filled with bottles containing bright coloured tablets and medicines; there were thousands, a junkie's paradise. No one else moved or spoke. In fact, my own voice sounded detached like it was echoing, and movements appeared to take more time than usual. It was almost like watching a film of me in slow motion. I remember realizing with a wave of triumph that I had all the drugs right there in front of me that I'd need for a grand exit. All I had to do was get away.

I must have walked pretty hastily out of the shop, but I felt like I was floating, and someone had hit the emergency button in the chemist shop, and alarm bells were ringing everywhere. They sounded deafening, and I was floating backwards out of the front door. The wind and light of the street hit me in the face as I looked around; no one stood between me and the cab. I jumped into the back seat of the waiting taxi, put the knife to the driver's throat and shouted, "Drive! Don't flash your lights, don't raise your arms, turn off the radio, and do NOT attract attention." We headed towards the M55, and as he drove, I set about emptying the canisters of drugs directly into my mouth. I was hurriedly opening bottle after bottle of morphine sulphate tablets, a few hundred in all. I snorted pharmaceutically pure BP heroin up one nostril; this set my nose on fire and brought tears to my eyes. I put the concentrated methadone powder up my other nostril, and the rest of the powders like morphine and methadone I emptied down my throat. I couldn't believe my eyes when I came across the Seconal and Tuinal, these were powerful barbiturates which on their own would be more than fatal, far more powerful than Temazepam or Nitrazepam, they'd been taken off the market a few years previously. I felt like a child in a sweet shop as I washed them down with two and a half litres of methadone. As the taxi drove down the road, I glanced sideways through the window, and I could see everyday people going about their everyday business. Their lives only hours before held a positive attraction to me, but torturing myself with this thought now seemed pointless. I remember thinking, *This is it, it's over.* Nobody could save me now. Not even God.

I gave the taxi driver the address of my parents' house, and as we drew close, I could hear police sirens in the distance. The drugs had just started to take effect like a volcano erupting inside of me. Nothing really seemed to matter now. All I had to do was just wait for the inevitable. I told the driver to pull up in the back street. When I left the cab, I asked the driver to give me two or three minutes grace before radioing the police. I left the taxi and staggered through the back gate into my back garden. As I came through the gate, my dad was pottering around in the back garden tending the flowers he so loved. I said "Hi," and he looked at me and smiled. He could see I was clearly in another bad state like many times before. I thought, *This will be the last time I see him.* I had a lump in my throat and found it hard to swallow. I nodded and walked past him through the back door and up the stairs to my bedroom. I got into bed and pulled the covers over my head and waited to die. Things were getting really hazy now, and I remember thinking over and over, *It won't be long.* A wave of warmth and tranquillity washed over me as the drugs now flooded my system, and I closed my eyes.

After a few minutes, I vaguely heard a knock at my bedroom door. I struggled to get out of bed, bouncing off the walls like an old wino as I reached for the door handle. I knew my life would change forever once I opened it, and it did. I saw nothing but police, all up and down the stairs, crammed in the hallway, all dressed in body armour, each one carrying a baton and shield. I thought maybe I was just seeing some endless progression, that it was all a bad trip. That was my last thought. I collapsed into nothingness, and I was told later that they had to carry me down the stairs and outside, where they threw me into the back of a waiting police van. I was falling in and out of consciousness. A couple of the police officers who were there said that they had headed off to the police station and that about halfway through the journey someone noticed that I'd gone blue and wasn't breathing. You would have thought they'd have radioed for an ambulance, but they just turned the vehicle around and headed towards the local hospital, that actually made more sense. We eventually arrived at the hospital where I was taken to the accident and emergency entrance. One of the nurses who had admitted me told me some years later that I "was the wrong shade of blue." As if there is a right one!

I was taken to the intensive care unit DOA, put on a life support machine with my mum, dad, and my wife at my side for four days; they only left to visit the chapel where they prayed for me and wondered where I'd gone wrong. They felt helpless and were clinging to any hope that I would survive this ordeal. They were obviously very aware of the events that led to what could be considered my deathbed, but their main concern was simply to have their son live. This was a terrible position for any parent to find themselves in, and I was totally oblivious. What an utterly selfish act, even though done in desperation. Suicide is a permanent solution to a temporary problem. I was driven by a force inside me to self-destruct that I didn't understand, but knew it could only be satisfied by either more drugs or death.

It wouldn't be long, however, until I would understand and deeply regret the impact of my actions on those around me. I'd put my parents through so much pain.

I had let them down badly, and yet this was in conflict with another part of me that desperately wanted them to be proud of me. I stayed on the life support for four days with the machine doing my breathing. On day four, one of the nurses noticed my foot move. I was gradually coming around from the drugs, and the first thing I recall is yanking at the tubes stuck into my body and sliding off the bed. I don't remember seeing anyone in the room, so I headed for the door as the police officer who was watching me had gone for a pee, I was later told. I made my way down the main corridor with my catheter dragging behind me, trying to look inconspicuous, and I met the same police officer who was now on his way back up to the room. I was immediately marched back to the ward.

It all was just a brief moment of consciousness before I blacked out again. My family had been warned not to hold out much chance of recovery. With the amount of drugs I'd consumed and the oxygen deprivation, they said I would probably never be able to feed myself or do anything for myself ever again. That would have been the worst scenario I could have imagined. I finally came around again in a small room at the end of the ward, while handcuffed to the bed and with drips sticking in me like a voodoo doll. All I can remember are the vague sounds of voices echoing around me, and as my vision cleared, I could see some sort of tube going into my chest. This was where my chest was cut open for speed as the doctors found it difficult to find a vein. The two black blobs in front of me morphed into coppers who now stood on either side of the bed.

I knew immediately that this wasn't the Pearly Gates since I figured I'd gone to Hell, but I knew there would be more heat coming my way.

I would now have to face the consequences of my irresponsible actions. I remember thinking, *This is so typical, I can't even kill myself properly*, followed by a feeling of relief that I really was alive. I was feeling very ill, though I'd find out later that I had pneumonia. The cuffs felt too tight, the future looked bleak, and I didn't think too much of the present company either. Finally, the doctor came around, and he told me I would be released in about a week. He didn't have to say anything more. I knew that after that I'd be going straight off to prison for a good long while. My first thought was that if I could only drag out my stay in hospital, then maybe I could escape. Common sense took over, and I realized there was nowhere to go but hospital when you're feeling this ill. It was like a dark cloud descending on me as the thought sunk in. But there was another thought that was driving out that dark one: I had survived. I wasn't meant to, but I had, and maybe there was a reason I was still alive.

I'd never seriously considered the possibility of change since my last stint in rehab. A series of past cock-ups left me with the mindset that change was for others, not me. I could change how I felt with drugs, but to tackle life clean was at this moment almost unfathomable to me, and I hoped the idea would grow on me. Drugs had been my magic carpet from one state to another; they were my getaway car to a better place to escape the pain and insecurities I felt deep inside me. I'd had a couple of friends who got off the gear and had changed. They had gone to rehab and were now clean, but I was sure that I was one of those people who weren't able to live without some sort of mood-altering chemical. Or rather this was what I'd deluded myself into believing, and once you start believing your own bullshit, you're in trouble. Now I was in it up to my neck.

It wasn't long before I needed the toilet, so we set off, me and my various attachments and the copper who was like my shadow, while I pushed my drip stand with the other hand and held my catheter bag. All the other patients were staring at me. I was allowed to go into the room on my own, at least, for which I was grateful. This was a trip to the toilet I'd never forget. When I finished, I looked down into the pan and saw that my shit was jet black. I went to the sink and looked in the mirror and saw that I had black stuff on my face from the nose down. I stuck out my tongue, and it was jet black, too.

I started to feel dizzy. All sorts of thoughts were running through my head: did I have bowel cancer or some sort of deadly disease? I caught myself in the mirror and saw a stranger looking back. My eyes had sunk into my head with dark circles underneath them; my complexion was like a waxwork dummy, grey. The police were now banging on the door, and shouting, "You'd better not be up to anything in there!" "Fuck off!" I shouted back. What could they do to a dying man? Then I heard a nurse shouting my name, "Phil, Phil, you OK in there, love?" I slowly walked toward the loo door and let the nurse in. I felt like I was rotting from the inside, and I needed help. I told her of my find in the toilet bowl, and she started laughing, which I thought was fairly insensitive. She informed me that all the black drainage was caused by my having been pumped full of charcoal to soak up the drugs. I struggled back down the hall with my apparatus. They took me back to my bed, and I immediately fell asleep. When I awoke the following morning, I looked around my room, and my heart sank. My police guard had changed. The copper who came on shift looked over to my locker and saw the chess set someone had placed there. "Want a thrashing at chess, lad?" He was a Yorkshireman with a big red nose who looked like he was in his late fifties. This man looked as if he could have drunk the equivalent of the English Channel in whisky. After beating him at chess for the third time, we decided to call it a day. He wasn't too fazed at my ribbing him and said he let me win because I was ill. Then it came, the lecture. "What made you do it son? How come you can't have a few pints like the rest of us?" The double standards thing was something I couldn't quite get my head around, and I was still off my face, so I came back with, "I don't want to go there, boss." The possibility that his liver could be in worse shape than mine made anything else he might say void. It wasn't all just a bad dream, then.

    The sun was pouring through the window, and I could smell summer in the air, and the dawn chorus was belting out a song of optimism. I loved to hear birds singing; however, I didn't share their mood. I was going nowhere but to a bigger, more hostile shithole. I could hear footsteps in the corridor outside my room and the muffled sound of distant voices. I fought off a wave of emotion, and something in the steps told me who was approaching. The door opened, and my mum and dad stepped in quietly, and as we saw each other, the tears began to flow. I'd be hard-pressed to explain what I was feeling; on the one hand, I was delighted that my plan to end it all hadn't worked out. Sadness mixed with guilt swamped me, and that familiar feeling of shame made it hard for me to lift my head. What had I done this time? It could have been the end for my folks as well. On the other hand, I felt deep sorrow and confusion concerning the future. I looked my dad straight in the eye when he asked how I was. "I'm fine, now," I said. My mum kept saying, "You're going to be alright. You're going to be alright."

"I don't know what will be happening to me, or how long I'll have to go to prison for, but I do know one thing for sure, I'm going to change." I'd started the conversation with real conviction, but as I got to the end, I realized how inadequate my words sounded. There just weren't any words I might use that would sound real.

"I know Phil," Dad said, and they both agreed and smiled. The smile stayed on Dad's face for a few moments and then faded. I'd never seen either of them looking so tired and worn out. I wondered how many years I had aged them. I could see the pain of my addiction chiselled on their faces. A voice inside me said, *"they won't be around forever, Phil,"* and I was flooded with guilt again, more so as my mum told me of their endless nights at my bedside, afraid to sleep, afraid even to run out for a bite to eat, so sure they were that they might lose me. They say that at some point, if you don't kill yourself first, you hit rock bottom, and the world suddenly looks very different. The obvious suffering on the faces of my parents. I'd never really seen it before, not in all its reality since my focus had always been on myself or gear. All I could do now was tell them that they *would* see a change in my behaviour; I would stop inflicting so much disappointment on them. If the words sounded more hollow than usual, then it was just one of life's crazy ironies, for I genuinely meant it this time, and I really wanted just to get on and do it, whatever the hurdles.

I waved goodbye to my parents as they left the hospital and asked them to give my daughter Sarah a cuddle for me. They said they'd be seeing her that weekend, and that she always asked about me. Sarah was now four years old; her mother and I had split up when she was two. She'd been taken into the care system not long after I'd left her mum, and she had spent the last two years of her young life in a children's home. What would happen to her now? I could see her beautiful face in my imagination. She had the whitest blonde hair with the bluest of eyes; they were like pools of clear blue water, and she had the smile of an angel. I'd called her Sarah as it means princess, my little princess who I loved very much, but I could not and would not show my feelings in front of the copper who had just now returned and was standing beside me. I loved Sarah so much, and I knew on a head level, I should be a responsible dad. Maybe now was my time to learn how to be a real father. Sarah's mum, Tracey, was still out there taking drugs, so I knew what I had to do. I just gave my mum a nod; I knew she'd understand, and they walked out of the room.

Next to visit was my wife. I'd not been looking forward to seeing her, and I didn't really know what I'd say. The minute she walked into the room, there were tears. She was standing over me dripping tears on the crisp white sheet, and I didn't know what to do, so I just watched them roll down her face.

"I'm sorry," she said finally. I mentally kicked myself for not saying it first. It was me who owed the explanations, not just for this last episode but also for the bad times that had come before. It was my entire fault; I could see that plain as day now, but before I could say a word, she beat me to it.

"It was all my fault, Phil," she said, and she scrunched her eyes and looked up at the ceiling tile with that begging, merciful look on her face I'd come to hate these past months. She looked at me like she was about to explode with grief. "I'm so sorry," she said finally, and the words started to fly out of her mouth. "I should have never kicked you like I did; it was wrong! And the things I said, I should never have said what I said, and . . ."

And the words kept pouring out, but I stopped hearing them, not because I didn't sympathize, but because I was suddenly hearing an entirely new voice inside of me. The voice was saying, "Ann listen, it's not your fault." Those words alone, when they came out, were like I'd exorcised some devil; my usual response would have been to make her feel even more guilty. But I knew deep down that my time for bearing grudges was finished. For once in my life,

I was going to take responsibility for what I'd done. I heard myself saying the words inside my head, and I finally even got them to leave my mouth. "It's OK, Ann," I said finally, "it's me alone that put me in here." It was a true enough fact and also the first time in years that I wasn't blaming someone else for my troubles. Usually, it was the typical villains: a probation officer, a judge, a prison officer or a drug worker, and when I couldn't find a person to blame, I'd just blame Margaret Thatcher and the whole Tory government. This mindset was a main link in the chain that shackled me to my drugs. No responsibility.

I got the words out, and then we both cried.

Time in the hospital went slow, and I wanted it that way; the food was good, and the company was good as I could talk to the staff. And after a couple of days, the police left my room and sat at the end of the hall, so I even had the run of the ward. I didn't want this last bit of freedom to come to an end, but I knew it would soon enough. It was pretty apparent that I'd be heading off to jail. After two weeks, I was discharged by the doctor straight into police custody, irony of ironies, with a big bottle of Methadone and another of Nitrazepam, though to my dislike they were handed to my police escort. I was hauled in handcuffs past the old man who had once worked with me at the tower circus when I was a ring boy, and he averted his eyes; past the nurses at the desk who stopped their giggling and started whispering instead; past the orderly who had talked to me about the Liverpool music scene but now just nodded; past people I vowed would never again see me in such bad shape.

Chapter Two

We left the glass and stainless-steel corridor, and they shoved me into the back of a waiting police car. I was still quite frail and also sick with fear as soon I would have to face my demons with no chemical walking stick. While I'd been in the hospital, my withdrawals were kept at arm's length by the Methadone; the doctor had said it was dangerous to have me strung out. Now the judge of this would be the prison doctors, who back then had their own alternative ideas about detoxing prisoners. The usual method involved moving you to the hospital wing and chucking you in a cell with no medication, just a piss bucket for company. You didn't see the light of day until it was all over, and some didn't see it again, period.

I was charged with robbery and false imprisonment. My cell door was opened and slammed behind me, and the odours brought back a flood of bad memories. I remembered the smells of stale body odour and piss mixed with lime; the air was thin, and all I could do was curl up in a ball on the mattress with my head in my hands and try to get some rest. The only thing I could hear was other prisoners shouting through their door hatch to each other and the occasional jangle of keys. I was due up in court in the morning, which I wasn't looking forward to. I knew there was little point in applying for bail, so I just wanted it over and done with. My family would be there, and it was just more pain for everyone concerned.

I lay stretched out on my mattress knowing it would be wise to get my head down; I was exhausted in every way. I woke up to a copper putting my breakfast on the cell floor. In a disorientated stupor, I desperately tried to focus on gathering my thoughts; my mind was still awash with memories of my dream. I'd dreamed I was a skittle on a bowling lane where authority figures from my life would take turns in taking shots at me. I was stood ridged as the balls thundered towards me, the sound frightening, but they all missed, and I was still left standing somehow. I didn't know if this was some unconscious prophecy or just the result of all the brain cells I'd fried over the years, but it wasn't welcomed as now I needed to concentrate as my solicitor would be here soon.

About an hour later, my cell door opened. A small but stocky copper with huge arms and a freaky smile told me that my solicitor was there to see me. He took me to another part of the station, stopping every few steps to get my prison issue slippers on properly. My groin ached; it was getting harder to get a hit there now, and my leg ulcers were on fire. When I walked into the interview room, I looked over to my brief, and I saw his eyes wide behind his thick-lensed glasses. I could see the shock register on his face as he looked at my physical state. I'd forgotten how rough I still looked. This man was a really good solicitor and was a very decent fella. This same man had fought my corner numerous times, and I trusted him. He tried to smile. "How are you feeling now, Phil?" "Like shit warmed up really," I replied, which broke the ice. Then thinking I might as well cut to the chase, I added, "How long does this sort of offence carry?"

"Well ... it's hard to say at just a glance, but taking a guess?

Ten years."

My arse almost fell out there and then. I had no more clever lines. "What?"

"Phil, you had a knife at someone's throat. You were robbing them. Then you've kidnapped a taxi driver. You ain't getting community service."

My head was spinning, and just at that moment, a copper came to the door.

"Grimes! You're next up!"

I was taken to a small holding cell under the court. As I walked in, I heard a voice say, "Fucking hell! Phil!" I turned to see a small, round-shouldered guy with long hair, seated on the metal bench. He was wearing a Bob Marley tee shirt, twelve sizes too big, and it took me a second to recognize it was Neil. A good friend from way back when. As the copper pointed me to a seat, Neil kept on chatting in a fierce whisper. "I heard your name on the radio for that chemist job in town. What happened?" he asked.

Not wanting to appear as gutted as I really was, I replied "Oh, I only nipped in for some plasters, and it all went badly wrong." Neil, as it turns out had been nicked for dealing, both himself and his girlfriend, and was expecting five years or thereabouts. Like me, heroin had not been kind to him. His years of drug addiction were clear to see, along with a huge black eye from a scuffle with the police.

My name was called, and I made my way over to the door, then up a flight of concrete stairs that carried me into a completely different world. We surfaced in the courtroom. The lights were dazzling, the room silent and warm, with the musty smell of a library, and a dozen or so spectators, probably family and friends, filled the wooden benches behind the dock. A reporter with bobbed hair and too much jewellery sat waiting for the details. Regret and remorse were laying me out, but there was no turning back. I spotted my mum and dad at the back of the court as I stood in the dock. I smiled to acknowledge them, and my dad winked at me. Mum gave a nervous smile; I could read right through that smile to the worry which lay behind.

I turned to face the magistrates, but I already knew the outcome. There were hardly any words spoken at all, just my name, and the charge was read out by the prosecution, followed by the matter-of-fact voice of the magistrate. As I expected, I was remanded in custody. I was taken back downstairs without even getting another glance at my folks. On my way, I nodded at Neil, who was next in the dock. When I finally got back to my bench, I lay down, made a roly and thanked the stars that court was out of the way for now. I thought best just chill-out and wait for the other happy customers to be dealt with.

We boarded the meat wagon about an hour later. The sun was scorching, and I could hear holidaymakers passing by on the streets, laughing and having far too good a time. However, in the sweatbox, we were all stuck in cubicles no bigger than small wardrobes, health and safety didn't exist when it came to transporting prisoners. We were definitely not off on our jollies, and the ride to Preston Prison was bumpy, boring, and plain miserable. As we pulled up to the big gates at the front, they swung open and swallowed us whole. "Here we go again." These gates would have looked right at home in a wall of the Tower, more a castle gate with an arched top. I could feel eyes staring at us from one of those top windows as we left the wagon, and I glanced up. The panes were dirty with bars behind. Through the bars I saw heads, then a face, old and wrinkled, wreathed by tangled grey hair and with eyes like a hawk about to plunge; he was an old wino I'd bought downers off occasionally. I hardly recognized him without his trilby, which had earned him the name 'Tommy the hat'. Tommy's stints in prison had definitely prolonged his life; his head usually glowed like a Belisha beacon, and the bright red traffic light look had now left his face, but his sense of humour and big smile remained. My thoughts were soon brought back to the here and now by a wrenching feeling in my stomach. The methadone that had been holding me was on its way out, and I knew this rattle would be one I'd never forget.

The thought alone made me sick. I looked for a place to part with my breakfast and started griping, but I had none to dump. I was freezing, yet the sun was beating down mercilessly, and inside the van, it had been roasting. I stepped down onto the concrete and watched the big gates closing, my last glimpse of the real world for a while. A screw pointed us towards the reception. The gate screeched open, and we were pointed towards a large empty room with stone walls. "Stay seated till your name is called!" shouted the screw with a strong Glaswegian accent, his voice echoing through the room. The stone walls had been washed with that institutional cream paint that always reminded me of a three-day-old mushroom soup, and I began to gip again.

We were waiting to be admitted; most men had resigned themselves to the fact they were in jail now and to chill for a while before they were called. One particular bloke was starting to look agitated. He had the wildest hair and beard I've ever seen on any man or beast. He'd started by pacing up and down the room, talking to himself in the strangest accent. This guy was clearly having a breakdown or had mental health problems. "Oi! What you in for, wild man?" shouted the Scouser next to me. The voice was so loud that the man managed to tear himself away from his own conversation.

"I shot Brian," he replied, staring at this Scouser, and for a second or two, everything went quiet. This was followed by a wave of laughter, and jokes started flying out. Jokes about Monty Python's *Life of Brian*.

"You shot the Messiah," somebody blurted out, and the whole room just cracked up. "Life for Brian!" somebody else shouted, and a short chant broke out, "Life for Brian," until wild man stared back with that glazed-over look and not the slightest bit of fear in his eye. "Fuck off," he said, with his nose an inch away from his tormentor's face. I remember thinking, *You got the wrong man on the wrong day to take the piss out of*. It turned out he was a farmer, and this was his first time in jail. The topic had now changed to shagging sheep and was just getting off the ground when

the screw shouted his name. The man jerked up and pounced on his cardboard box holding all his possessions, grabbed it, and strutted off through the iron gate. I was relieved for him; it would only have gotten worse, and he was already close to flipping.

The entertainment now gone, it seemed like an eternity before my name was called. The reception screw was called Jonesy. He was of a small build, a bald Welshman with buck teeth and a manic laugh that would make any psycho proud. He had the kind of face that looked really lived in and only a mother could love. I hadn't noticed him earlier as I had entered the reception. I'd worked for him before in the prison stores on another sentence. He was quite a funny guy who complained endlessly about either his mortgage or his mother-in-law, but at the end of the day, he was an alright bloke, but he remained a screw, and I never got too familiar with them.

"What are the charges," he said. He was smiling like he was auditioning for the film *Deliverance*.

"Robbery, false imprisonment," I said.

"What happened in court?"

I thought that was a little bit too obvious to answer, and I resisted the urge to say, "I got bail, boss, didn't you know?"

"Remanded in custody, boss," I replied. He nodded and turned to the filing cabinet. Then I went through to get a shower. Showers were the best part of the process as far as I could see, and I couldn't wait to wash off the shit and dirt from the police cells. The stream of water was fast and hot. It almost felt like I was washing the dirt from my soul.

I towelled off and then went back to the desk where they returned to me my jeans, tee shirts, and trainers. I wasn't about to wear prison issue until I had to. I knew from past experience, it was made to fit giants and dwarfs, no one in between.

Next, it was off to see the doctor; I waited outside his door for my name to be called. I walked in, and there was this tall bloke seated behind a desk, along with a hospital screw wearing a white jacket. His face was bright red; he was sporting a big yellow dickey bow, a tweed jacket, and a pair of those half-moon glasses that sat on the end of his nose. This could not be the doctor. This had to be a *One Flew Over the Cuckoo's Nest* extra. I stood there saying nothing; the silence was deafening. Then he rose up from his paperwork and looked me in the eye. "Not going to kill yourself are you, son?"

"No, Doctor, tried that one, and it didn't work."

"Good, well you are off to the hospital, as you're not well." I saw he had a name tag. It read, "Dr Gordon".

Once all twenty-plus of us had been processed, we were taken to a steel and glass door at the end of the reception. The line hesitated for a moment while the enormity of that little opening settled on the group; it was the door through to the main prison. We were marched through the door and were hit square with brilliant artificial lighting. Suddenly, there were no shadows. Then a nasty smell from the recesses invaded my nostrils. It may have been bright, but it was still a dump, and you still had to slop out, queue up and to empty the contents of your piss bucket in a slops sink. The smell of shit and ammonia could make your eyes water.

Then there were the common noises of steel doors slamming and men getting banged up, the jingle jangle of keys and empty voices ran as background noise, all of it echoing through the steel and stone of this old Victorian institution. As I walked further along the wing, I happened to look up through the safety netting which seemed to hang there like a spider's web waiting to catch those unlucky enough to fall or jump off the top landing. I could see my old cell five floors up and was flooded with memories.

I liked it up there because I could see over the wall into the town. I saw myself all those years before, on the day of my release, with my bedroll under my arm, full of gate fever, mixed with relief that I was going home after three long years behind the door.

Eventually, a screw in a white coat came up the stairs and led us down to what's called "The Ones". The perfect sewer for the medical observation ward, where we were all but lab rats. It was about as far removed from a hospital as you could ever imagine — a more unsterile place you'd struggle to find. Prisoners called it Fraggle Rock; I suppose because it had some similar looking characters as the kids' programme. A landing full of square pegs trying to exist in a round hole. Fraggle Rock was a place that reminded some of the more seasoned cons of their own mental instability, and the fear of losing it. I'd heard rumours of guys in prison losing the plot, then sectioned under the Mental Health Act, ending up on a landing like this.

"Down in Fraggle Rock," as the song went. A lot of men were there for psychiatric assessments for court; others had experienced a nervous breakdown while serving a sentence. You could almost taste the desperation and helplessness in the air, along with a powerful stench of food slop. The only other thing that qualified a man for Fraggle was a murder charge. *Fuck this*, I thought. "I'm only withdrawing off drugs; I've not killed anyone, yet," I said to the hospital screw now looking at my charts. He didn't bother to look up at me, but he wrote a sentence on another chart. My objections were falling on deaf ears; it was clear he'd undergone an empathy bypass. I was starting to feel dizzy when he handed me a plastic measure with one Valium and two paracetamol. I downed them and chased them with water and waited like a seismic sensor for the tiniest unwinding the drugs might bring — I should be so lucky. I was led to a cell down the landing. The screw opened it up.

"Behind your door, Grimes, quick!" I stepped in, and the door banged shut.

I didn't take another step; I just stared around at the place. It wasn't fit for human habitation. There were blood and shit all over the walls and even on the ceiling. I was later told that someone had slashed their wrists there.

"How does that happen when you're on observation?" I'd asked, but there'd been no reply. I knew the answer to my question: simple, no one gave a fuck.

The bricks were painted light blue and again covered with stories of Jimmy from Bolton who got life, and Dave of Preston who got stitched up by the police. Someone had vomited in the corner, and it had run down the walls. The slop bucket, now my very own toilet, stunk like it was from the abyss, and there was hardly any air or light getting in through my window. Every now and then, you could hear the sickening soft thud of shit parcels being thrown out of the cell windows above; it landed in the dirt outside the window. I finally stood on my pipes to reach my window with the thought of closing it tight as the air coming in was rank, but it wouldn't close.

I left it open and looked over to my bed where there was only three-quarters of a mattress. It was the final straw. I was already on meltdown by that time, and I pressed my bell and banged on the door for twenty minutes or so until I heard steps and a voice outside the door.

"Bang on that door again, Grimes, and you'll be going in the strip cell!"

"It's got to be better than this fucking hole!" I shouted back, so I banged for about another five minutes but to no avail.

In the end, I had to stop. I'd started to feel dizzy and let go of my stomach's last remnants into the bucket. The smell only made me feel worse, and I collapsed on the lump of mattress in a heap. I was burning up and freezing at the same time. I'll never forget feeling the sensation of ice running through my bones, instead of marrow. My stomach was cramping up as I'd been sick that much. It was almost like I had a snake writhing around inside my stomach, and the whole first day was spent crawling back and forth between the bed and the piss bucket. I'd never rattled quite like this before. I kept saying to myself, it's got to end sometime; instead, it got more intense. And after what I'd put down my neck from the chemist alone, I shouldn't have expected any less. Add to that my years of drug taking, my body was bound to be a wreck.

Thoughts were racing through my head at an alarming rate; you can't do this so kill yourself and have done with it. Even if you get clean, who will want to bother with an ole junkie? You're a piece of shit for the way you treated your family. Do everyone a favour and put a rope up to the bars. I could see in my mind's eye my little girl sat on her bed in the children's home asking staff, "Do I still have a daddy? Where is he? How come he hasn't come and got me?" I could only sit there with all this and cry.

As I reflected on my situation, it was right out of a social work textbook: my daughter was in a children's home; I had no educational achievement, and I'd caused my family tremendous stress and pain, not to mention the fear I'd put my victims through. My brief told me to expect about ten years, and here I was rattling my tits off. In the cold light of day, though, things could have gone the other way for me. I could be in the morgue with no second chance and a name tag tied round my big toe, yet now I had this spark of hope inside of me which was there one minute and gone the next. I didn't know much else other than lying, stealing, hustling, and getting wasted, but I could learn. I realized there's a lot I needed to change about myself, and I had to keep taunting myself with the thought. If I could get through this, I could get through anything life could throw at me. The only other option was to go back to drugs like a dog returning to eat its own vomit. It was now pitch black, and I felt exhausted. I would have paid anything for a few hours' sleep.

It must have been the early hour of the morning, and by now, I was feeling distressed and exhausted. My head was all over the place. I found myself on all fours throwing up. I still had the suicidal voices telling me to get on with it, and really enough was enough. It was at this point I decided to call out to God. So with vomit still hanging from my mouth and drenched in sweat, still on all fours, I said, "If you are real, and you love me, here I am. Help me, Jesus. You can have what's left of this life, make yourself real to me."

My only experience of church was as a kid at Sunday school, other than that I had once called into a local church and injected in their toilets. I had generally found Christians either a bit weird or stuck up; however, the idea of a bit of one-to-one time with God was now more than ever appealing to me.

I felt a warm energy surge through me, and momentarily my thoughts cleared. I thought, *Wow, this is actually real*. It seemed like this experience lasted minutes, but in reality, it was about an hour, then it all came thundering back.

Chapter Three

I was born in Blackpool in Glenroyd Maternity Hospital, 1961, a true Sandgrownian, which is someone who was actually born in Blackpool. A small seaside town in the north of England, where the majority of its visitors, when I was growing up, were working-class people who came in their swarms and packed the beach, its piers, and the town's amusement arcades and bingo halls to part with their hard-earned cash.

    I come from a working-class family. My dad was a Yorkshireman, a joiner, who was a well-built man of about six-foot in height. He was a kind and gentle man who never raised his voice to anyone. He was laid-back in his nature and earned the name 'Gentleman Jack' years later and wasn't one to rush into things. He would make me things out of wood and was always slow and methodical, a perfectionist who never made mistakes with wood in his hands. When my dad made something from wood, it was built for life and would never fall apart or break. He made me stilts, and once made this cart out of an old seesaw; one of the things I loved about this was I could fit all my pals on it. He would spend hours making things as well as bending six-inch nails in half with his bare hands to keep me amused. I'd shout, "More, Dad, more!" I was as proud as hell of my dad.

My mum, Margaret was a very good-looking lady with shoulder-length brown hair. She was only 5 ft 2 inches, slim build, and the matriarch of the family. Mum would dance to the Beatles and the Dave Clark Five and other music of the 60's. We had a large radiogram, and I'd bounce around next to her. She would make me cardboard guitars with wool for strings. One day, Mum bought me a kid's guitar, and I strummed it until I had blisters on every finger. I was a typical boy who never sought trouble, but somehow trouble would search me out!

My earliest memories of childhood were around three years of age. I was at a friend's house playing with a ball, and my ball rolled under a couch. I went to retrieve it and did so with a Jack Russell attached to the end of my nose. My yellow jumper quickly became a red one, and I was taken up to hospital to get it stitched.

There was an old couple who lived next door to us, my Uncle Tom and Auntie Ethel. I would help him with his much-loved garden, pulling up weeds as he pruned his roses to perfection. His lawn was so well mowed you could have almost played bowls on it; in fact, bowls were his favourite pastime. When the rag 'n' bone man had been around with his horse and cart, he would have me follow it down the road carrying a shovel until the horse decided to take a crap, at which point I'd scoop it up using both hands and take it back to Uncle Tom to throw around his precious roses. My reward for doing this was half a glass of Mackeson brown ale filled up with lemonade to make a nice cool shandy. Sometimes he'd be over-generous with the brown ale, which made me feel good. Even back then I guess I was learning how to get my kicks, not even realizing what was happening. I couldn't wait for the fish cart or rag 'n' bone cart to come back around.

I have a sister who is five years older than me, called Julie. Like lots of brothers and sisters, we got on some of the time and rowed and argued the rest; the usual sibling rivalry, yet if anyone older picked on me, Julie would be there to defend me. Julie was a tomboy who loved animals. She had mice in the coal shed, hamsters in the garden shed, and a Shetland pony which was kept close by, the first of many. Thursday night was a time we both looked forward to, treat night. It was the day our dad got paid. He flogged his guts out from six in the morning until six at night on building sites, and the joiners' shop for ten pounds a week. He would arrive home with a big bag of sweets and chocolate, offcuts of firewood from the shop floor, collapse into his chair and watch *Top of the Pops* on our old black and white television in front of a roaring fire.

I was about to start school soon so went into town with my mum to get a uniform. I tried on a brand-new pair of shoes and a pair of grey short trousers. I thought the shoes were the best thing ever; the tread was made up of animal tracks, and inside on the heel was a compass. Not that I knew how to read one. I didn't think that much of the short trousers and wondered if we could one day afford long trousers.

The big day came. I was taken to Waterloo Primary by my mum, quite unfazed on the journey, to this old, grey-looking building. My parents had sold me the idea by telling me there'd be lots of other boys to play with. It wasn't until my mum had to leave me in this large hall that I began to feel frightened. I stood there wearing my school cap, blazer, jumper, short trousers, grey socks, and my new black shoes, with a piece of card which had my name written on. It had been punched on at either side and threaded with wool then hung around my neck. It was then that the tears came. There were these huge teachers collecting kids into groups then sending them off through these large wooden blue doors, none of which looked happy about their fate. After a short time, this very tall older woman with grey hair scraped into a bun took me by the hand. She led me through one of the large blue doors into a classroom. School broke up the boredom of being at home all day, but even so, I have to admit I was not sold on the idea. It seemed like a necessary evil that all kids of my age must tolerate. My first couple of years there were quite easy, and I especially enjoyed music and art and craft-type lessons.

One Friday afternoon, the teacher had organized us into groups of four. We had to agree amongst ourselves a play, which was to last for about ten minutes, then act it out. There was a kid in my group called Richard; he was larger than the rest of us, taller and broader with a thick crop of ginger hair. He somehow always managed to have an angry look about him, and he looked dishevelled in his appearance.

That day, as school was over and we were all getting our coats, he came over to where I stood, grabbed hold of my collar and said, "Listen you, I want some money off you on Monday, or you're dead!" I remember my heart racing as I wondered what I could have done wrong to upset him. I went home that night with this in my mind, worried about what would happen on Monday. By the time my dad got home, I must have looked a sorry state as the first words out of his mouth were, "What's the matter, Phil?" After much debate I spat it out, asking, "What do you think I should do, Dad? After a long pause, he said, "Well, Phil, sometimes in life, if you can't beat them, join them," and he said no more, a man of few words. I knew he wanted me to stick up for myself. This would mean having a go back and fight this lad who seemed twice my size. I'd stuck up for myself a few times on the street, but this lad towered over me. I thought about what my dad had said and came to the conclusion he must be right; after all, I had seen the advert on television for Tetley bitter men, which clearly states if you can't beat 'em, join 'em.

The weekend seemed to go extremely fast, and Monday morning soon came around, and I had no money for Richard. It was break time, and I was engrossed in a game of marbles with my friend, Mick, when Richard approached me. "Where's my money?" and he booted me in the shin. As the pain exploded in my leg, he thought that was enough and stepped back, so I punched him on the side of the head. He was surprised that a squirt of my size dare even retaliate, but it didn't do me much good as he had me wrestled to the ground in seconds, punching me in the face. He now had the upper hand and said to me in his squeaky voice, "If you can't bring money, you'll have to fight him," and he pointed at Mick. So Mick and I had to fight. The rules were no one was allowed to give in until he said. So Mick and I knocked the shit out of each other most days after school for roughly about twelve months. Richard came up to me one break time and began winding me up, showing off to some girls, and then he hit me. I don't know that much of what happened after that, other than the headmaster pulling me off him as I was banging his head into the concrete. My twelve months of sparring with Mick had stood me in good stead, and I was told later I'd pasted him; he would never bully me again.

I was caned for this by the headmaster. This must have been the most enjoyable part of his job as he never smiled otherwise. I was determined not to show any fear or pain on my face, although I was shitting myself. He was a formidable-looking guy with a huge nose, was really tall, and weighed about nineteen stone. Mr Smith had short, cropped hair, big sideburns, and usually wore a dark suit. His big shiny black boots squeaked with each step he took. He made me promise that I would be a good boy from then on.

Not that long after this fight with Richard, we were both in the toilets at the same time, stood side-by-side in what was a red brick open-air toilet. I was minding my own business, watching my jet of pee hit the urinal when I heard a shrilling scream in my left ear. I turned to look at him, his eyes full of tears that fell onto his cheeks and rolled onto his shirt. His screams got louder, and on a closer examination, I saw he'd got his dick caught in his flies to the point where his mangled-up manhood was pouring blood onto his already shaking legs. He shouted, "Help! Help! Get the teacher, get the teacher!" By now I was laughing and said, "I'll get the teacher, Richard, don't move." Not that he could, he was fixed to the spot with pain, crying helplessly. So I walked back to my classroom laughing and said nothing to anyone; every few minutes, I smiled to myself and laughed inwardly.

It was about ten or fifteen minutes later when he hobbled past the classroom window with the deputy headteacher, still crying. I thought, *That's good enough for him; he's made my life hell.*

I stopped paying attention in class and began fooling about. School was boring, and this was much more enjoyable, and it made others laugh. This attracted attention; the wrong kind of attention, and it wasn't long before I was back before the headmaster for a caning once more. He said I was stupid, not really very nurturing comments to an impressionable kid, then gave me the cane good and proper this time. If anti-bullying policies had existed back then, he would have been the worst culprit; I was nine years old.

I continued mucking around and fell really behind in lessons, eventually getting put into what was known as the dunces' class, where we all struggled with similar things, and everyone was naughty. It was great as we were left to fool around, and our teacher said very little. He was an older man in his late fifties called Mr McDonald. Occasionally, he'd try to re-focus the class by shouting "Grimes, you blithering idiot, what are you doing?" This seemed to be his reply for everything, to which I'd taken to replying with old McDonald's farm. We were taught ITA which was a way of spelling words phonetically, then after a couple of years, you were expected to forget what you'd been learning to then use the Queen's English. I just couldn't get my head around it.

Once I'd walked through the school gates, I never gave the place another thought. Home was a safer place, and with plenty of things to do like experimenting with my dad's homebrew. In our garden shed were demijohns full of sherry, elderberry, and blackberry wine.

My sister, Julie, had started smoking and went to the shed so that she wasn't caught. The shed was at the bottom of the garden. My dad kept some of his work tools in there and firewood; Julie kept her hamsters in there, and although it was cramped, it was our den. Once, when I was in there, she asked me if I wanted a drag, probably covering her back against future blackmail attempts. She passed her fag to me. I took a long hard pull on the cigarette and swallowed, as my face changed colour, and the smoke hit the bottom of my lungs, I thought I was going to choke. Even though the nicotine made me feel dizzy, I was curious enough to ask for another drag. I thought, *It must have been me doing it wrong,* but I got the same result again, this time coughing till I thought I might burst a blood vessel. My sister was enjoying her smoke, as well as laughing at me, so I wondered that if I persevered, I'd enjoy smoking too. I didn't realize I was creating a life-long habit that I would transfer onto other drugs in later years. A couple of my sister's friends came over, and we let them in, and as the smoke wafted out, our attention soon turned to the homebrew. Since my mum had taken a job as a shop assistant, it meant both my parents were out all day. I'd either go to my gran's for tea or my sister looked after me. We wondered how grown up we'd look with a drink of sherry and a fag, so Julie ran to the house to fetch a couple of glasses. I poured myself a glass of this dark rich brown-red liquid, the smell of fruit so powerful. And I took that first gulp as it trickled down my throat into my stomach, making my senses do summersaults. It seemed only a couple of minutes until I felt the heat in my belly rise up through me like watching the temperature rise on a thermometer; it had now hit the roof. I'd watched the cowboys in the westerns swig it back, so I raised the glass again, threw my head back and finished my glass. It was only when a few more minutes passed that one of the first things I noticed about the new changes within me was how confident I was now feeling, nothing seemed to be quite as serious now, I thought. Julie and I giggled and said, "Grown-ups drink this all the time, and it does them no harm." In total ignorance, a door was opened deep inside me, and the key to lock it back up was missing.

    I had started knocking about with a lad from the next street to mine. Glen was two years older than me yet was still the same size; he had a pale complexion and curly brown hair and always had an anxious, shifty look about him. He appeared to have quite a bit of money for his age, and he smoked. He called this one day and asked if I was coming out, so I got my coat, and we left. We made our way to the corner shop and bought five Park Drive and a book of matches costing five and a half pence. The man who served us looked straight at us and told us he sold cigarettes in singles in case we were ever short of money. When we got outside, we looked at each other and laughed. "What the fuck was his game?" When we got around the corner, Glen said, "Here, Phil, I've got you this." He went inside the tartan lining of his Arrington jacket and pulled out a load of chocolate. I was well impressed! "Where d'you get that, Glen?"

"Oh, I nicked it from the shop just then; didn't you notice?"

"No, I replied."

"Well, neither did he," said Glen, shoving it towards me. I hesitated at first, looking behind me to see who was around. We laughed again and carried on walking. We walked a bit farther to some garages that were behind my house; there were a couple that had been left open. Inside, it was dark, our voices echoed as we shouted, "Oi, oi, oi!" I didn't like the dark as a kid so thought lighting a fire was a good idea. We smoked our cigarettes and ate our chocolate with our small fire burning and crackling. I could see the flames dancing in Glen's eyes. It had started to get fiercely cold, and the streetlights were now glowing like orange beacons against the sky. We sat and talked about our next visit to the shop; it was now my turn to nick something. I'd soon get my chance to prove myself as a thief.

My opportunity came a few days later. We were in the shop buying some singles, and Glen winked to me indicating that he was keeping the shopkeeper busy, so I filled my pockets with my eyes fixed firmly on the shopkeeper and the entrance. I loved the buzz and excitement of nicking; it felt good at the time, the thought of getting caught, not so good. No one would find out if I kept my wits about me; it was our secret.

A few days later, Glen and I were off to get some conkers from what we called the posh side: these were some large houses about half a mile away. It only took us ten minutes to walk. When we arrived, I put my canvas rucksack on the ground. We had seen our tree a couple of days before. It was down a small alley at the side of this large house, and if we climbed the big wall, we could reach plenty of conkers. So up we went; this tree was enormous, so we decided to take it in turns. It was on about my third climb when I thought we had enough conkers now. I'd just get this last clump at the end of the branch. It was when I was halfway down the branch that I heard the branch creak, and I was accepting my fate when gravity sealed it. I fell ten feet, still clinging desperately to the branch. I crashed through the asbestos garage roof below onto the roof of this big posh Jaguar. I was unable to breathe at first and thought that judging by the crashing sound and the dull thud of my body hitting the car, I had to be fatally injured, but no, it had knocked the wind out of me. Apart from cuts, bruising, and a very sore back, I'd live.

Glen was unable to open the up-and-over door. I was trapped, so off he went in search of help. I sat waiting for his swift return. An hour later, I was looking up through the hole I'd made in the roof; I could see the blue sky and fluffy white clouds and the occasional seagull making its way to the sea. Next, I heard, "Phil you still there?" "Yeah get me out." Glen had brought his older brother, Terry. He was bigger and stronger than us, so he set about yanking on the garage door. The door screeched its way open, and the sunlight blinded me for a couple of seconds, then we heard "Oi, what you little bastards doing?" We ran for our lives with this bloke of about thirty legging after us down the road. We knew the back streets like the back of our hands, so we ran down one, across some spare land, and we lost him. As we gasped for breath, we laughed. "Who the fuck was that? He'd never catch us." We thought we were safe as houses until Mr Angry showed up again screaming, "Come here you little bastards; I'm gonna ring ya fucking necks!" The chase was back on. We tore down the street and headed towards a back alley; we turned into the alley, and I was oblivious to the mongrel taking a crap and went arse over tit with the dog. I don't know what was worse, the thought of this guy catching us or the smell of dog shit from my sleeve which was also smeared on my hand. We continued running with Mr Angry in hot pursuit. Glen was now laughing at the dog shit incident; we couldn't run for laughing, and the gap was closing. We decided to go in different directions. I raced down a couple more streets and decided I would take my chances and hide under a parked car. I could see Mr Angry's feet as he circled the car saying, "Where the fuck have they gone? I'll kill the little bastards!"

    Days had passed since our conkering expedition, and I called around for Glen at his auntie's. He was going to see his dad on the Golden Mile if I wanted to go. He told me his dad owned a bingo and amusement arcade on the promenade, and we could play the machines. We played the fruit machines all afternoon then went for a drink in the staff quarters. Almost in the middle of this room sat his granddad, behind a table filled with money — more money than I'd ever seen. I mean it was loaded. Piles of change and other coins waiting to be counted; piles of notes and others that were scattered around. There was even some that had got knocked onto the floor. We got our drinks then went to talk to his granddad. Another employee shouted over, and Granddad was distracted. Glen whispered to get a note off the floor, and we'd go to the Pleasure Beach. I bent down swiftly to pretend to tie up my shoelace. I grabbed a five-pound note, screwing it up and tightening my hand around it. I looked about to see that no one had clocked me; we were safe, so we made a hasty retreat, laughing and daring each other to nick more next time. After doing all the rides and stuffing our faces with burgers, we agreed that we'd do this again.

After repeating our routine, and en route to the Pleasure Beach again, we bumped into Glen's older brother, Terry, who was on the street with his mates, drinking cider. We changed our plans rapidly to go with Terry and his mates to have a drink in the park. The cider was dry and fizzy in my throat, and when we'd drank enough to get merry, Glen asked his brother if he'd go to the off-licence for us to get our own cider, and we'd share it too. When he arrived back, we passed the bottles around. As we drunk more, I was looking at the world from the big wheel now, and everything went round until the sky and the ground melted into one. It took me the rest of the afternoon to sober up enough to go back home to face my mum and dad; I made an excuse to go to my room and crashed out on my bed.

Glen and I continued nicking money from his dad's arcade, two, sometimes three times a week. It was easy money, and we'd got really good; as one of us distracted either his granddad and later on his dad, we took what we needed to buy our QC cream sherry and Strongbow cider with the aid of his brother.

Life carried on as normal at home; my mum and dad hadn't noticed I was drinking yet. I was quite skilled and devious at covering my tracks. I guess the biggest disappointment for them were my school reports which turned out to be chronic. But as I was soon due to leave junior and start secondary school shortly, maybe I'd do better with a fresh start.

Chapter Four

My first day at my new high school didn't get off to a good start as I'd missed my bus and rolled up ten minutes late. I was greeted by two prefects looking very serious. It was their job to take the names of latecomers. Things got decidedly worse from there on in. I walked down the long corridor with its shiny floors; kids were rushing around trying to find their classroom, and some were glancing at their timetables anxiously. There was a strong smell of sawdust in the air, and the lighting was dim. I found my classroom, taking a few deep breaths before I put my hand on the brass door handle. *How come everything is so shiny*? I thought. With some apprehension, I pressed the latch and walked in. All the other kids were now settled and acquainted with the new teacher; I didn't feel right in this place. Come to think of it, I always felt different from the others, not better, far from it, just different. "My name is Mr May." I stood there looking lost and slightly bewildered for a few seconds, when the teacher approached me. "What's your name, son?" "Phillip Grimes, sir," I gulped. "Oh, so you're Phillip Grimes." His size tens were now planted firmly on top of my feet. I thought, *How does he know about me, how could this be*? He continued with "Well, Phillip Grimes, how is it everyone else got here on time, and you didn't?" He was now punctuating his every word like a robot and poking me in the chest with the tips of his fingers; they were ridged. I thought I would fall backwards but was determined not to, but with him now crushing my feet and pushing me backwards with each stab of his fingers, this was proving to be difficult. I could feel myself getting angry so knew I had to say something, even if it might not have been the right words. I shouted at him, "Fucking get off me yer big twat, fuck off, fuck off!" I knew of my destination the moment the first expletive leapt from my mouth and into the atmosphere, but he was now hurting me. He pushed me out from the classroom, up the concrete stairs outside the headmaster's office. "Stand here!" he yelled, his voice now losing its pitch and his face beetroot red. He was a youngish man, in his twenties with beady eyes which his glasses magnified, and he had an athletic build. Outside the headmaster's office, I was now feeling really frightened, pretty lonely, and quite sorry for myself. I got distracted looking at these fantastic paintings that had been done by others from the art department, now hanging on the wall as a reminder that this was what good students produced. I stared at one which was a ship on a stormy sea. I loved the colours and detail and was wondering what the outcome would be of my own personal storm. I made an inner vow to myself that day, outside that room: *No way am I going to co-operate with these teachers if this is how I'm going to be treated*. What would happen if I did something really bad, would it be a matter of time before another teacher tried to put me down in front of a class and make me look like a twat? At that precise moment, the door swung open.

I got a distinct waft of pipe tobacco and the headmaster's Old Spice aftershave before I actually saw him. "Come inside boy and stand here. We will not and do not tolerate lateness, let alone bad language!" I would have said or agreed to almost anything to avoid the stench of stale coffee on his breath. He leaned even further forward and said, "You are here to learn!" At this point, I could see all the fillings in his mouth — not a pretty sight. I looked at his collar, as I didn't feel comfortable when screaming adults were so in my face. "And do as my staff tell you! Do you understand, my boy?"

"Yes, sir."

"This is your first warning on your first day; this isn't good, Grimes; however, because this is the first day of term and I'm feeling generous, you won't be caned on this occasion. Now get out of my sight, and remember, Grimes, I never forget a face, and I don't want to see yours again, now get back to your class." So I turned and headed back to my classroom.

As I tried to settle into my new school, I soon found out that the teachers weren't the only people I had to worry about; there were some of the other kids too. Most of the kids at my school were from the council estate just down the road. A small group in my class was terrorizing a kid from another area; they were a tight-knit bunch and were rarely apart. I wondered how long it would be before they realized that I wasn't from around here too. There was no way I would just stand for it like most of these other kids were, these bullies were making this kid's life a pure misery. I felt quite sorry for them but knew better than to stick my nose in. I'd served my apprenticeship under Richard, and if anyone came bullying me, I'd at least have a go, even if I wasn't going to win. It didn't take the bullies too long to work it out. One day, after school, as I was walking home with my mate minding my own business, I found myself surrounded by four older kids with angry faces. The biggest one, with the biggest mouth, got hold of my hair saying I wasn't allowed to walk this route home. I shouted to Pete who I walked home with to leg it, and he was gone like a whippet. This kid yanking my hair was really hurting me, and before I knew it, I was lifted off the ground. They'd picked me up and slung me over a hedge into a load of muddy water in someone's front garden. I sat there for a moment soaking wet, shit up to the eyeballs, thinking, *You wankers I'm going to get a real bollocking when I get in, thanks to you lot.* Next to where I lay was a rusty metal stake that I'd landed on. I grabbed hold of it and stood up. It felt solid in my grasp and weighed a few pounds. I could see these lads across the road still laughing about what they'd just done to me. As I walked, my feet squelched with my every step from the water now in my shoes. I couldn't hold myself back much longer; I was far too angry. I ran straight into them swinging my stake and screaming, "Come on, then!" As I heard the thud of metal against skull, I knew it would cause damage just by the sheer weight. It was the big kid, with the big mouth. I should have known by the enormous scream he let out instantly as he squatted down to stop himself falling flat on his face, deep red blood trickled down his face and neck. His friends ran off up the road to watch from a distance. I threw the stake in some bushes and legged it, leaving this kid bleeding and crying on the pavement. I remember thinking, *I hope he doesn't have to go to hospital or I'm in big trouble.*

I squelched my way up the garden path and opened our front door hoping no one would be in. Mum took one look at me and went ballistic at the state of my uniform. It was her day off, and now she'd spend the rest of it cleaning my clothes "I fell on my way home, honest, Mum."

"Get to your room and get that uniform off, now!" Mum was screaming now, and this was always a good indicator she was at her wits' end with me.

My auntie had got me a job at Blackpool Tower. She was a manager in the catering department. At twelve, I was sick of school already. I thought it made far more sense to have money in your pocket, so I worked after school between 4–6 and at weekends 9–6 for eight pounds a week. I loved working at the weekends in the Tower Lounge; I was tucked away in the kitchen of a burger bar. One of the things I enjoyed about this job was having a laugh with the waiters, who'd bring me a pint of cold lager to the kitchen. They had access to alcohol, and I had an endless supply of burgers and sandwiches, so we struck a deal. On my breaks, I would wander off to watch some of the acts in the tower circus as there were just two doors separating it from where I worked. I loved the excitement of it all, the beautiful horses, and the smell of the other animals, the bright colours in the special lighting, and the half-naked women in their skimpy costumes. The music from the orchestra made the trapeze artists' every move all the more dramatic, and I appeared to enjoy everything all the more once I'd got some alcohol inside me, so this was great. I'd sit in my seat watching the acts, daydreaming that one day when I left school, this would be where I'd work. I would sit there watching the ring lads run into the circus ring and set up the props, and because it was dark, I could count all the money I'd fiddled; none of the stock was counted.

Back in school, I was getting into fights, trouble with teachers, and being generally unruly. The only thing the teachers seemed to be able to engage me with was music. I played clarinet and saxophone and enjoyed music. I could barely read and write, but I could read music quite well, and I found it easy as I thought in pictures and could pick out the notes clearly.

I found the best thing to do with the money I was earning was buy records: David Bowie, T Rex, and Jr Walker & the All Stars. I was playing truant quite a lot and loved to sit in my bedroom and escape into my music or roam the amusement arcades playing the bandits. My older sister wrote me notes to hand in at school; she'd got quite good at Mum's signature, and I was amazed as it was a complicated squiggle.

I was thirteen and drinking either after school with Glen most nights or at the Tower whilst working. There was a girl at school who I was told fancied me; her name was Julie, and she was the head girl. By using her friends as go-betweens, we arranged to meet me at the shops at six. It was quite a cold night, and it had started to rain, so we went and sheltered around the back of a nearby junior school. After a few minutes of fumbling around, I lost my virginity. She was older than me, and more experienced, of which I was glad, as it was a case of the old dog teaching a new dog tricks.

I started to get the symptoms of being run down; I got lots of sties in the corner of my eye; apparently, this is what you get when you are washed out, and I wasn't sleeping well. I would lie awake under my covers listening to Radio Luxembourg, while the rest of the world slept. So I was taken to see the doctor. It was a rainy day, so I said to my mum that I'd run in on my own; this was nothing unusual as I'd gone in to see the doctor on my own before. He asked me how I was feeling, how I found school, and if anything was worrying me? My doctor was of the old school; he was a plump man in his fifties, always friendly. He wore a hearing aid yet talked very loudly; his fountain pen was on automatic pilot. He said he was going to give me something to help me sleep and some ointment for my eye. When I got back into the car, sitting down on the cold leather seats of our old black Riley — I called this car the Batmobile — I told Mum I'd got some pills for my eyes and some ointment because they were, weren't they?

That night, I took one of these capsules. I loved the effects; it blew my head off, so I took another two. This rocked me nicely.

Four weeks later when I saw him again for an update, I told the doctor they didn't work; out came the good old fountain pen, and he gave me something called Mogadon.

These made my head feel like it was full of marshmallows, very relaxed, nothing really mattered anymore. The only downside was that everything I ate tasted the same, like cardboard. I soon worked out that if I took enough of these tablets, I could get a better buzz than drinking. Another bonus about taking pills was there was no smell on your breath as with alcohol when encountering adults.

I was wagging school one day in an arcade; it was throwing it down outside, so I'd taken cover until it stopped. I was playing on my favourite bandit, I liked to play this one because the lights mesmerized me, and I loved the noise it made when it paid out. I always thought I'd got one over on the machine when it paid, and it was a brilliant feeling scooping up my winnings. Another couple of lads who looked about fourteen came over and watched as I played the bandit. We got talking about wagging school, and how only mugs went to school. Someone once said that education is expensive, but ignorance costs more. The lesson I was about to learn would cost me dearly.

Jason was the more streetwise of the two. He was a big lad with long blond curly hair, a large round face, and a ridiculous laugh. Alan was the quieter one. He was tall and thin, with short dark hair and a tooth missing at the front. They told me that they had been pinching his aunt's slimming tablets and were going camping; they had endless energy and stayed up all night talking. Not exactly my idea of fun really, but when I told them about the tablets I'd got, they asked me if I'd swap some with them. Jason told me that his dad took these slimming tablets all the time, and they made you feel fantastic.

I said I'd meet them back at the arcade the next day.

I took five of these orange tablets, which looked more like Tic-Tacs than anything, so I didn't expect much to happen, they were called Filon. That was in the morning; it was five o'clock before I realized the day had gone. I was hypnotized by the bandit and had an immediate bond with these two kids I'd only just met the day before. Everything was much more interesting than usual. I felt like I could do anything, say anything, go anywhere, be anyone I wanted; I felt fucking amazing!

A couple of months had passed before I returned to see the doctor, this time all by myself. My nights without sleep were affecting my concentration, as well as my attitude. I told my doctor of my troubles, and he prescribed me these capsules called Tuinal 200 mgs. I had never heard of the term barbiturate back then. Not realizing these were the most powerful sleeping tablets known to man, I headed off to the chemist. That night, I couldn't wait to try these new pills. I sat in my bedroom listening to some Bowie, drinking a cup of tea with two of these capsules in my hand. They were as light as a feather, and I loved the colour; one half was bright blue, and the other was bright orange. The hit off these barbs was amazing. I felt confident and complete on the inside. All fear left me, along with other insecurities; it was like I'd had alcohol, but it was far superior and far heavier. I was in a trance-like state where time didn't exist. I was hypnotized looking at the posters on my wall, and my music was now far more interesting. *This is what it's all about.*

How come everyone didn't take Tuinal?

I'd started drinking with a mate from school, Pete. We'd drink in his bedroom when his parents were down the club. He lived not too far from our house, just up Central Drive, and this Friday night, I was staying over at his. We went down to the snooker hall in the town centre and had a few games. I'd taken my Tuinal and was nicely tuned in. On our way home, we laughed about this old bloke who showed us how easy it was to rob bandits. All we had to do was bend some metal where the change return was, then using a tail comb, keeping hold of the plastic end, touch a switch inside and it would pay out. We could empty the machine doing this and decided to go to an arcade the next day and try this out. We talked about how much money we could make as we walked up the terraced street to his front door. When we got in, I dropped another couple of downers and went to bed.

It must have been early in the morning, as I stirred in my sleep. I was completely out of it from the Tuinal, but something must have bothered me as I opened my eyes. Pete's older brother was sucking my cock whilst I slept; it took a few seconds for the situation to register. I grabbed his hair and banged his head on the bedroom wall. Adrenaline kicked in as I sunk my fist into his horrified face. I was screaming, "I'll kill you, you cunt, you fucking bastard!" His parents rushed in, and when they saw what mess their precious son was in, they started screaming too, "Get out of this house!" I got my clothes on quickly, and when I was just about to leave, I turned to his dad, "I didn't know your Steven was a fucking weirdo. I woke up to him sucking my dick, the dirty bastard."

His mum screamed again not wanting to even consider the implications of my accusations, but his dad had gone very quiet as if he knew something his wife didn't. I started walking home, feeling dirty. Maybe it was simply my fault, and I deserved it, even though I'd done nothing wrong. Feeling ashamed of myself and very angry, I continued down the road plotting my revenge, "I'll do that dirty bastard first chance I get. He will pay," I said to myself. I walked in the house and reached for my downers, then jumped in the bath. As my drugs filtered through into my consciousness, my magic carpet took me to a better place away from my feelings of self-disgust. I'd become quite skilled at changing the way I felt by taking one mood altering chemical or another to get into whatever desired state; this day I ordered some oblivion. Next day, I was back to the doctors to order more of the same, more downers.

A friend of mine who lived on the next street, Tony, asked me if I wanted to go with him to the casino on the Pleasure Beach — there was a soul club there on a Friday.

I'd been in the place about fifteen minutes and bumped into Jason and Alan from the arcade, "Got any more downers, Phil?"

"Yeah, a few Tuinal."

"What! How did you get those?"

I tapped my nose. "It's not what you know, it's who you know." We laughed. He gave me a few of his auntie's slimming tablets, and I gave them some downers; we all had a drop. We sat talking with some girls until our drugs kicked in. I'd been really enjoying myself listening to the northern soul and talking crap. Over the other side of the club, we heard shouting and banging. It was Glasgow fortnight, really busy, so we thought nothing of it at first. Then the sound of breaking glass as it shattered above our heads and landed on us grabbed our attention. Jason shouted it's off, come on Phil, let's give it 'em," so we pushed our way over to the door. It was like the Wild West, women screaming, loads of pushing and shoving, and bottles and glasses flying at us and over the top of where we were. We eventually made it to the top of the stairs where the fight was happening. The music had stopped, now there was only shouting. The next thing I knew, this huge guy came running at me screaming, "I'll fucking kill you, li'l bastard!" I didn't too much fancy the odds here; I was only fourteen, and this guy must have been twenty. More out of fear than anything else, I picked up this big heavy ashtray and flung it at this guy's head. It was more luck than judgment, as I first heard the thud and then saw the blood as it shattered on his forehead; a roar went up from the Blackpool lads who'd seen what had happened. His screams were now drowned by those still shouting, and the amount of blood was sickening. His white shirt now covered in deep red, this guy staggered off towards the door staff; he didn't look a pretty sight. This was my David and Goliath moment; although I was just fortunate I hit the target. Word got around about this incident, so the next time I was invited to go along with the lads who'd initiated the violence, they told me it happened every week if I was up for it. And sure enough, it did, with firms from all over the country most weekends.

I loved the adrenaline buzz and excitement of violence but gravitated more towards my drugs, and the idea of risking my liberty without a financial gain wasn't really resonating with me. My recreational drug use had now escalated into dependency, and if I didn't take my downers, I felt shaky and anxious. So I took more of them, more often, and speed at the weekends. My drinking continued, and when I didn't have drugs, I'd be plotting a way to get my hands on some.

I was 16 now, and like all kids of that age, what I didn't know about life wasn't worth knowing. I knew best, and after all, I would live forever. I was about to be proved completely wrong with this kind of thinking and attitude, to the point where the more I learned, the less I realized I knew.

I had agreed to go to another soul club with Tony the following week at Wigan Casino. I'd told my parents I'd be sleeping at Tony's, and I'd see them the next day.

We walked from Tony's house to catch the train. We were really looking forward to this; we'd heard all about the all-nighters at Wigan and how the place was flooded with drugs. As we arrived at North Station, there was a small group of people standing around outside. I got talking with this lad who was speeding his face off, called Kev. His eyes looked as though they would involuntarily burst from his head at any moment; he was in his late teens with a puckered complexion which made him look older. Kev was a very thin guy, wearing Birmingham bags; his three-quarter-length leather coat hung from his wiry frame, homemade tattoos defaced his hands.

This world of drugs and its characters was becoming ever more appealing to me; after all, those things in life with the strongest pull have the forbidden fruit element to them. It had an attraction I couldn't quite understand, so I never attempted to understand it, but just got ever more sucked into its dark vacuum.

Kev told me he'd been using drugs for a couple of years now, and if I wanted the ultimate hit, he had some white stuff in his pocket. It had come from a chemist that had been screwed and was as rare as rocking horse shit. Straight away I said, "I'll have some."

"It'll cost you a fiver, or if you just want a hit, it'll be a quid, follow me to the bogs." I went with him to the toilets, and we went into a cubical. "Have you got a works on you?"

"No," I replied, not really knowing what he was on about and not wanting to appear thick at the same time. He pulled out a 2-ml syringe with an orange spike. I gulped and said, "I've never done this before."

"Oh, it's OK, I'll get you a vein". Anxiety was starting to get the better of me, so I said, "Go on, be quick." The needle broke the skin making me tense up, and drawing back the plunger, dark red blood almost mushroomed into the barrel. As the plunger made its way towards the tip of the works, I felt warmth wash over me along with that big dipper feeling as it steams down the first hill, the one where your stomach doesn't belong to you anymore. My face, particularly my nose, itched like crazy. As I looked around the toilets, everything was at a distance, and the sinks appeared half a mile away. I had the opiate taste, as well as the smell through my nostrils, and beads of sweat glittered on my forehead. I didn't feel sick, and then my stomach did a summersault; a jet of vomit burst from my mouth, just missing Kev, hitting the mirror now in front of me then shooting back covering my brogue shoes. My clothes were now soaked in sweat, but I didn't care as a dreamy calmness had taken over me. Nothing seemed to matter anymore. The fact there was piss on the floor, graffiti on the walls, and I had blood running down my arm was inconsequential. This was to be my faithful magic carpet that took me places only I could go, away from the reality of a harsh world. Peace and security were now mine; there was an emptiness that I felt deep inside, but now the void had been filled. I looked out at the world now through different eyes; my perspective had changed, and things would never be the same again. Heroin had permeated my every cell, and this was how I'd have liked to remain until old age caught me, and I died. Tony walked into the toilet looking shocked at the state I was in. It didn't take too long before his curiosity had him with his sleeve rolled up. We missed our train to Wigan Casino, but there would be other days.

Back at Tony's place, we spent the rest of the evening in his bedroom waffling utter nonsense as we tried to come up with words to describe our new experience. The best I managed was: a million orgasms multiplied by infinity, words were not sufficient.

My sister was now pregnant, and her boyfriend, Billy, had moved into our house until they got themselves a flat. Billy was a builder who also worked the doors at weekends. We got on OK, and I liked his sense of humour.

Billy's other side-line when building work or door work was thin on the ground, was burglary. I shimmied up drain pipes and climbed through small windows for a small cut when Billy went on his night-time manoeuvres, breaking into shops and other premises. I was leaving school soon; maybe I could earn a living as a burglar?

The time came to sit exams and plan for the future. I felt really uncertain since I'd spent my time at school either dicking around when I was there or bunking off. I thought there was little point taking any exams. So I left with no qualifications under my belt.

Chapter Five

It was 1977. The Sex Pistols had released "God Save the Queen", so I spiked my hair, put on my silver bondage trousers, a destroyed tee-shirt, and painted my Doc Marten boots luminous green. I loved the idea of anarchy, chaos, and destruction; it really appealed to me as it was an accurate description of my life, thus far. I was drawn towards music and fashion, which deviated from the norm. Punk was the perfect vehicle for me to act out my frustration and aggression. I had developed a powerful hatred towards anything establishment. There was back then considerable resentment and feelings of hate towards the police in '77. The main source of this was the 'stop and search' powers the police overused or the (sus law) as it was known; to add to this your chances of getting a good kicking down in the cells were remarkably good. So you had nothing to lose by getting stuck into them as you couldn't make things much worse. Another constant cause of concern was that there were no audio recordings of police interviews, only handwritten accounts, written by the police themselves. This turned out to be a factor in many miscarriages of justice, given my experience.

I was now breaking into doctors' surgeries to steal prescription pads. I knew this Irish guy, called Joe, who seemed permanently smashed. To look at Joe, you could be forgiven for thinking he'd walked off a cowboy set. His hair was black and long with an overgrown goatee, and the lines etched deep into his face told a story of disappointment, rejection. He was a dab-hand at forging scripts. Joe was a highly intelligent man, who if he'd focused his attention towards a university degree or maybe business, I'm sure he could have been a massive success. He was one of many highly intelligent people who took drugs to escape the pain that existed in reality. Yet the wit and the skills that he employed to finance his drug habit and for survival were nothing sort of remarkable.

So, once I had the scripts, he'd write them, I'd cash them, and we'd share them. It was a good arrangement all around 'cause we all got smashed. We were getting large amounts of Diconal, Palfium, Mandrex, Tuinal, and Durophet. Morphine-based painkillers were the cream of the drugs scene, stronger than any street heroin you could find. As a consequence of this, the withdrawals were horrendous. My policy would be to use whatever amount was in front of me at any given moment. I had now also started to inject the Tuinal I was prescribed and loved the heavy rush; it left me like I'd been on a drip of the best Scotch whisky.

However, my tolerance to barbiturates had now become higher which meant I had to take more each time. My appetite for drugs grew to the point where they now dominated my every waking thought; I had to have them. I still worked at the Tower, and even with my fiddle, I still needed money to finance my drug taking. Crime seemed like the only sensible answer, so the more hands-on experience I actually got, the better I became. The other knock-on effect was that little voice in the back of my mind telling me when I was doing wrong got quieter and quieter. This meant less guilt and minimal fear, always a bonus when breaking in to anywhere.

I'd been out to a different soul club in the town, not too far from where I lived, The Mecca. The Mecca was a massive nightclub; it was bursting at the seams with holidaymakers.

That night, I took one too many Nembutal and remember leaving the Mecca with my mate, Dale, and that's all. The following day, I woke up still feeling wobbly. Dale was curled up in a sleeping bag under the window snoring away. I made my way downstairs making sure I held tightly to the handrail. I turned the corner to see my mum in the kitchen. I smiled and said, "HI, Mum."

On closer inspection when I looked at her again, I could see she'd been crying. "What's up, Mum?"

"What's up? I'll tell you what's up — you and your druggie mate upstairs."

"What do you mean?"

"Last night, your dad and I had to get out of bed; a neighbour phoned when they saw you and Dale flat out unconscious on the pavement, asleep in the torrential rain. You've been taking drugs, Phil, we know!" I didn't ever consider preparing myself for this moment and wished I was somewhere else. "Your dad and I brought you both in, dried you off, undressed you both and put you to bed. Why are you doing this to us? Your dad and I love you. Last night frightened us. We thought you were dead; we don't ever want to see you like that again. We will pay for you to see a specialist of some sort to get you sorted out."

"Mum, last night I'd been drinking."

"There was no smell of alcohol on your breath, and besides that, I have been told about the drug taking at The Mecca, so don't even think about lying; why Phil, why? We don't deserve this."

The 'why' question hung heavily in the air. I thought, *I wish I even knew why.*

This was the million-dollar question. Why did anyone take drugs? It certainly wasn't a conscious choice that I'd made to hurt my parents intentionally. All they had ever done was to show me love, nurtured me, and wanted the best for me.

I came to the conclusion I must be a bit thick. No one in their right mind would put a needle in their arm, in return for pleasure. And after all, hadn't my teachers confirmed this to me? This must be right; at the end of the day, they were educated. On reflection, I now wonder how much their comments influenced my direction in life.

At the time, I actually believed this to be true. It wasn't until years later that I realized this was how I had apportioned blame, to let myself off the hook. Anyway, this belief of mine worked and allowed me to continue my drug taking. It was true I hadn't been an academic giant at school, but I was intelligent and far from being thick. My only problem was that I was the only one that didn't know it. And if someone had told me this was not the case, I would not have believed it. My low self-esteem would not have allowed such a praiseworthy comment.

My mum had stopped crying now and had put her coat on. "I'm going to your grandma's." Slam! The door closed, and she had gone. I was glad because the guilt and shame of seeing her cry over my drug use were crushing me.

I shot off out through the front door the minute I knew Mum was out of the street and scored some drugs.

Morphine always seemed to put things into perspective and is a great leveller. I found it easier to look at situations with emotional distance; my feelings really were the most inconvenient of things, but now things were really out in the open, I had to deal with that.

Chapter Six

My first real taste of employment was a government Y.T.S scheme for the young and unemployed of the town. Blackpool's main source of employment was in the tourism industry and so was mainly seasonal. This was and still is seriously underpaid work. However, this scheme promised full unemployment benefit and twenty quid on top. We were sent out in groups of four with a supervisor, to paint and decorate the homes of elderly people. At the weekends we'd pile on one of the buses that were organized by Frank, a friend who owned a local record shop and travel to gigs at Lancaster University. We'd get to see most of the top punk bands of that time, usually with a fight thrown in for good measure.

When you signed up for the painting course, you were expected to attend college. This turned out to be my downfall. I wasn't going back to school for anyone, so along with a group of roughly ten, we'd go around to Scottie's house, drink beer, and play cards. On one of my visits to Lancaster to see The Clash, I bumped into a good friend of mine, called Lee. He was a tall, wiry guy, full of tattoos, with a big smile. He had recently been released from borstal and was hunting for a job. "Eh, Phil, I've heard that the Tower Circus are needing ring lads, you fancy taking a walk down tomorrow?" I loved the circus and had watched the ring boys at work many times, so I arranged to meet up with Lee the following day.

We walked through the Tower staff door and were directed to a basement which took us right into the circus ring. There were a few men sat on the ring fence laughing and having a crack. One of them slowly stood to his feet and approached us; with a huge outstretched hand, he greeted us.

"Hi, my name's Nick. I'm the ringmaster here." I immediately regretted shaking this man's hand, although physically he was not much to write home about, he had the strength of ten men. Nick was in his fifties, bald, wore theatre make-up and was extremely well-spoken. "Well lads, when can you start? I'll give you a week's trial, and if you can do the job, we'll look after you."

"Tomorrow Nick," we both replied.

"Come and meet the lads then; we have two crews, you'll both be in Micky's crew. Your job is to set up the props for the artists. We have a large cage to erect for the lions and tigers, then there's a big net for the trapeze artists. Oh, and by the way, you roll the pedestals in for the elephants; you'll get the hang of it." I remember thinking this is potentially dangerous stuff. Lee and I knew Micky and his three brothers but hadn't noticed them in the ring. "Micky will show us the ropes," Lee whispered to me. The men sat on the ring fence looked hard and wary of any newcomers into the circus. All of them were heavily tattooed and physically fit, probably in their early twenties, except one who was maybe thirty-odd. They were dressed identically in the circus uniform, red tee-shirt, blue trousers, and trainers or Doc's. It looked like a fairground workers' reunion.

That evening, Andy and I met up with Micky in the Ramsden Arms, and he told us the score. This didn't sound like work to me, although I knew it would be exceptionally physical.

The memory of a full-grown African elephant charging towards me after I'd rolled the pedestal into the ring still haunts me. I had practiced rolling this huge metal frame for two hours prior to the show with not too much success. The trick was to tilt it on its axis, balance it, and then roll it by feeding it through your hands.

We were waiting in the entrance with these heavy pedestals, waiting for the music to change, as that was the cue when suddenly I felt something touch my arse. I nearly dropped the pedestal when I turned to see this massive grey elephant nudging me with its trunk. It wanted to make me that little bit more nervous before I made my debut. I could hear laughter coming from around the corner and knew straight away I was the cause of amusement. The music changed, and I set off into the circus ring; immediately, I was faced with hundreds of wide-eyed holidaymakers. I remember thinking, *What's so fascinating about four blokes rolling big round things?"* I lost momentum with my pedestal, and it wobbled away from me, nearly taking me with it. I could hear more laughter now. Then it nearly came to a stop as it fell towards me. I finally made it to the spot where it was to go and dropped it down with much relief. It was then that I saw this huge elephant, about three foot away from me, and it kept coming, as I was next to its pedestal. I leapt over the ring fence landing on an old lady's lap. I didn't realize it was me the audience was laughing at. Micky and the rest of my team stood at the entrance to the ring doubled over. I got to my feet, and they'd disappeared. My embarrassment was not yet over. I went back to where I was told to stand at the entrance to the ring when someone shouted "Taxi!" I stood there thinking, *You won't get a cab around here mate*, when Nick pointed towards a box with a handle on the top. On the top of this red box was a hand brush. This time, Nick shouted "Taxi," pointing at the ring. I looked across to where the elephant, who nearly cut my life short, was now taking a crap. Norman came over and said, "Phil, whoever is closest to the taxi goes in the ring and sweeps up the shite." I could hear more laughter from backstage as I made my way across to where this elephant had crapped and was now finishing off. I was quite relieved the lights were slightly dimmed as I'd cheered up now, and my face glowed with embarrassment. I stood with my hands on my hips waiting and tapping my foot, pretending to whistle. I swept up these huge balls of shite which weighed a ton. When it looked like it would do more, I was gutted and just wanted to get back to our dressing room. One of the other ring lads ran into the ring, grabbed its little tail, pumped it up and down like you would an old-fashioned water pump, and another piece of shite dropped down. The crowd loved this and were laughing and clapping. At that point, we took a bow, picked up the taxi, which now weighed something like a suitcase, and I made my way backstage.

Now that I was working on a regular basis, I thought owning my own transport would be a good idea, so I bought myself a Honda Two-Fifty trials bike. At least I'd be at work on time. My dad came with me to the shop whilst I sorted out the HP and stood as guarantor. Then away I went on a brand-new bike. I loved this bike; problem was I loved my drugs just that little bit more, and bikes and drugs don't really go together.

My mum and dad had arranged for me to see a shrink privately regarding my drug taking. He was a guy in his late thirties, who worked from his home, which was a huge detached property in Lytham, a very wealthy area. At the beginning of my appointment, he started telling me all these really crap jokes, then he got up, walked over to this picture on the wall, and just stared at it for what seemed like ages. In the end, I laughed to make him feel better as it was becoming awkward and embarrassing. Then because I laughed, he said, "See, Mr Grimes, you're obviously not depressed, are you?"

"I never said I was, Doctor." This was a pointless exercise, as the man was clearly bonkers. My diagnosis was that this doctor needed drugs himself to shock him back to reality. It ended up him telling me this long boring story which I'm sure had some sort of point to it; only problem was, I wasn't getting it. What a waste of hard-earned cash.

There were no drug services in my town back then, so the next place I was taken to was in Manchester (Prestwich), where the doctor informed me of my fate if I continued down this path of drug taking. *Big deal, Doctor,* I thought, as he told me war stories of his other patients. My youthful arrogance prevented me from hearing what he was trying to say to me. Everyone he told me about was either now dead, or minus an arm or leg. Since I still had all my limbs and was breathing quite well on my own, I dismissed his accounts as scaremongering.

I was still using morphine, Diconal, Palfium, and Heroin when I could get it; the more I could get, the better. In between all of this, barbiturates filled in the gaps.

I had gone to visit a friend who didn't live too far from me. Rob was a laid-back guy with blond hair that had started to recede. He had recently lost his mum to cancer and had taken to blotting out the pain with a variety of drugs. I asked him if it was OK to have a hit, and I turned him on to some downers. Rob was a solid guy who could be relied on in a fight, also if the police showed up. The phone rang so Rob went out on business. I climbed the stairs to go for a crank in the toilet. I drew up my gear into the works. I'd decided to give my mainline a rest and rotate the veins I was using, as the track marks on my arm were starting to look a mess. I chose to go in a vein down near my wrist, which I'd used occasionally. I welcomed the sensation as the smack burst into my bloodstream and seemed to hit me right in my chest, causing me to take a deep breath. With my eyes open, I noticed the works still jutting out from my arm; a smile crossed my face. There was still gear left in my works, and I didn't have to think twice about what I would do with it. I still had my belt wrapped around my arm and thought it might as well stay there for now. I pulled the plunger back, and the barrel filled up. Still heavily stoned from my first hit, I pushed the plunger down quickly as I wanted the rest.

Immediately, a burning sensation shot up my arm to my head, then it turned into electricity as it continued down to my toes. "Fucking hell!" I screamed in total agony. This current of electricity wouldn't leave me alone. I very suddenly became aware of an immense throbbing pain in my wrist which became unbearable. As I looked at my hand, it had gone a dull grey colour. As I clasped it with my other hand, I realized it was starting to go cold. By the time I'd got downstairs to the front door, it was black, freezing cold, and didn't feel like it belonged to me. I had managed to put my crash helmet on by now and climbed on my bike. My problems seemed intensified as it was impossible to pull the clutch in now that half of my hand was dead. I had to get to the hospital rapidly. I knew this was serious, and I could lose my hand, so I phoned a taxi. I could work out how to pay later.

I walked into the casualty department at Blackpool Vic, roughly around six o'clock and booked in. After waiting for what felt like a lifetime, I approached a male nurse to show him my hand. My index finger, middle finger, and my hand down to my wrist were now black and freezing cold; the heroin in my system didn't even touch the pain. This nurse was in a rush somewhere as I'd stopped him. "What's the matter, son?"

"My hand has gone dead and very painful."

"What's happened?" So I told him I was having a hit and ... it was my first encounter with the NHS as an addict. "Well, you'll just have to go wait like everyone else." His attitude was surly and offhand, and he was now looking at me like I was shit on his shoe. An hour and a half later, I'd had enough, so I pulled him again. "Can someone take a look at my hand, please?" He put his nose up in the air and waddled off down the corridor. At this point, I pulled a doctor who was passing. "Doctor, can someone take a look at this, it's so painful?" I couldn't believe my ears when he came back with, "It's probably bruising, who've you hit?" All thoughts of logic and reason long gone, "I've not fucking hit anyone, yet. I need medical attention for fuck sake; can't you tell — what's your problem? I'm not asking you to like me — I'm asking you to treat me!" I heard a voice behind me, "Watch your manners, son." I didn't turn around but watched as the doctor swanned off down the corridor. "Dirty junkie," he whispered under his breath. The voice from behind spoke again, "I think it's time you left — now!" I turned to see a copper motioning for me to leave, so I showed him my hand. "Look at this," I said, hoping to appeal to his better nature; it fell on deaf ears. I walked out of the hospital not knowing what to do, so I jumped into a taxi and went home.

It got to about 2 a.m., and the pain had intensified even more, so I called out my doctor. I had already explained to my mum and dad what I'd done; I think they were still in a state of shock when the doctor arrived. Mum was crying, and Dad was looking rather concerned when I recounted the tale to the doctor. If the look on my doctor's face were anything to go by, I'd probably be dead in the next hour. "Phil, I will take you up to A&E, grab your coat." We walked into the hospital which was now full of the usual Friday night casualties. A guy, who'd been glassed in a nightclub was sat there holding his face together with a piece of lint. I sat down next to his girlfriend, who was crying her heart out. It's amazing the care and concern that comes your way when you have a doctor in your corner. Within minutes, I was put on a stretcher, had a drip attached to me, then told by the porter, who appeared to know more about medicine than any doctor, I would probably have my hand amputated the next day as I was getting wheeled off to a ward. I took a couple of barbs and drifted off into nothingness.

The next day, I woke to see an older doctor in a white coat looking at my hand, "How are you feeling, young man?" This was novel, a doctor who appeared to genuinely care. He felt my hand which now felt like a piece of meat that had been in the fridge overnight and said, "First of all, let me give you something for the pain." The morphine was a bonus that made me feel half human at least. "OK, Mr Grimes, we want to give you some anticoagulants and keep an eye on you. If they don't work, then I'm afraid you may lose your fingers, possibly your hand. I will give you tablets for the pain." He gave me Diconal, usually reserved for cancer pain, which made the hospital feel like a better place and numbed some of the pain. They also rigged me up to a drip-type device. This was a metal box with a huge syringe in the middle which was on a timer. This thing ticked like a bomb, and it looked like a bomb. And if I went anywhere, so did my bomb. Its purpose was to pump anticoagulants into me to thin my blood to dissolve the clot.

Later that evening, I'd started to get slightly bored. Time had started to drag for me now, mainly due to the ticking from this irritating drip reminding me of every passing second. I had passed some time talking to a guy opposite who hadn't eaten for two weeks, due to his stomach ulcers. He had swapped his obsession from alcohol to talking about food and what he'd eat when he was better.

I decided to go and make a break for it and go to the off-licence for some much-needed refreshments, to break the monotony. I made it past the nurses' station, giving them the most innocent face I could muster. I crossed the dual carriageway, holding my drip. It had started raining, so I was eager to get my booze and get back as my dressing gown, pyjamas, and slippers were now soaking wet. I returned to my ward totally undetected with my bottle of whisky. I sat in the day room, put my feet up, and got drunk, feeling like I'd actually achieved something.

That same evening, I lay in bed, off my face, whilst my barbs started to creep up on me. I was tranced out, staring into space when a man with two heads walked past me. I shook myself. *Phil, be calm, you just watched a guy with two heads walk in the smoke room*, I said to myself. *Better go and check this out*, I thought. I opened the door to see this poor guy in his twenties with a lump on the side of his neck that was level with his shoulder. I sat there listening to the story of how his lump had taken three days to grow. I found it difficult, as we talked, not to talk and look directly at the lump, instead of him. We'd been chatting for about an hour or so, and I'd been flicking my ash through a window above my head. When I brought my hand down, I could clearly see the normal colour returning. So much so, I went and told the nurse. She marked my hand with a pen where it was still black and told me to go and put my hand back in the air, so I did. By eight o'clock the next morning, my hand had returned back to its normal colour, apart from my thumb at the first knuckle. The doctor was due round shortly, so I could show him the improvement then. I lifted my hand so that he could see the improvement, and he seemed almost as happy as I was. On closer inspection, he turned to me and said, "Phil, we are going to have to amputate your thumb at the first knuckle tomorrow as you have gangrene in it. But this is a massive improvement because I was coming to you today to inform you that it would be your whole hand!" The following day, I went down to the theatre, and they took off my thumb at the first knuckle. My first thought when I came round was, *How will I roll a fag now*? But I'm sure that was the anaesthetic. My attention shifted to the man with two heads; he'd gone down to theatre just after me, but there was no news as yet. It was only a couple of hours later when I saw his wife and her mother; I found out he'd died on the table.

Chapter Seven

It was Saturday night. I made my way to meet some friends and to wait for our coach, which would take us to Preston to see a band (The Vibrators). When I arrived in the town centre, there were about twenty punks sitting on the steps of an old church, drinking, laughing, and talking about the possibility of trouble with the Preston lot. Punk gigs were sometimes a place for unfinished business from the terraces and Blackpool v Preston was our local derby, so there was a very good chance blood would be spilt, and there was a real sense that tonight would be serious. I went to sit with some of the lads from my area, where the talk turned towards tactics. There were people getting on our coach who we didn't know and maybe couldn't be relied on if things got ugly so we would stick together whatever 'cause we'd be seriously outnumbered. I'd been to quite a few Preston games at Deepdale, which usually resulted in a fierce scuffle, but tonight's situation appeared to have a different element to it. We'd be locked in a building with them, and there were no coppers. The journey to Preston was like any other trip to a footy match, with plenty of drink, drugs, and chanting. As we neared Preston, our coach started to get pelted with missiles. We approached some traffic lights, and before we knew it, there were about twenty Preston lads booting the side of the bus. There was a loud hiss of hydraulics as the driver opened the front doors for us to leave the bus and pile into these Preston lads. Much to our disappointment, they ran off, so we dived back on our bus. As we walked to the venue, there was a large crowd at the front door where you'd pay to get in. It opened up like the Red Sea, people backed away, they knew that we weren't from Preston. Once we'd paid, we made our way in to see a couple of hundred people already in the auditorium. The atmosphere was electric, and all my senses were pumped.

Now seemed like a good time to get a drink, so I made my way to the bar. I had taken some barbs on the way down, so I was feeling quite mellow under the circumstances. I necked a couple of pints in the bar and made my way back to where our lads were stood at the front of the stage. The support band had been playing for about five minutes; their name summed up their musical ability to a tee. The Depressions were not going down too well! One of our lot, who I was standing next to, thought things needed livening up, so he leapt forward onto the stage, grabbing a microphone and screaming, "Seasiders!" at the top of his voice. Our mob from central Blackpool was at the stage front, the rest were scattered around the auditorium. This changed everything. The response was immediate as chairs started to rain down on us from upstairs. We fought a long and hard battle that night but got our arses kicked, as we were outnumbered massively; it was survival of the fittest. Stood between our lot and the door, which was the only exit, were roughly a hundred

Preston lads, and twice as many outside. The feeling I was now trapped descended on me, so I ran into them thinking, *Fuck it, I'd sooner do something about the situation than feel like this.* The first thing I encountered was getting punched by this student bloke full on the nose. He caught me a 'good un', which blurred my vision for what seemed like ages. I couldn't see anything, so I kept throwing punches in what I thought was the direction of the door. I knew I'd connected a couple of times but was now getting hit from all angles. I retreated back into a space, to see one of our lads get knocked on his arse, so I ran over and pulled him back. It was then I thought I heard Big Ben chime, along with a sharp pain in the side of my head. I staggered sideways, almost falling over the fire extinguisher that had been wrapped around my head. There were still scuffles going on all over the place, but now I couldn't hear anything as my ears were still ringing as though Big Ben was now in my head.

When it was all over, blood soaked my top from a wound above my eye and a bust nose, and now the police were streaming through the door; some had dogs, others were shoving people up against walls as the fight continued. Just as I thought it was all over, I clocked the student who broke my nose. He looked like he could have been my probation officer's twin brother, with long curly hair and a big beard. I thought, cop for this you twat and kicked him square in the bollocks. I was glad the connection was sweet as he was a big guy, so I punched him a couple of times in the head with my fist.

As the dust settled, a young man lay dead on the floor. The police rounded our coach party up and escorted us back to the bus, as they did so we walked from the building; we all looked in horror as we passed the body. Now out on the street, a shower of bottles, bricks, and lumps of wood was thrown at us by a mob further down the road. Once back on the coach, we were driven to the police station and taken off one at a time to be interviewed by the police. I learned later there were four or five statements that had been made against me — three were made by people I didn't know, and two were girls who'd travelled down on the coach. Sometime in the early hours of the morning, I was charged with affray.

Eighteen of us stood in the dock at Preston Crown Court. The old Victorian courthouse had been designed specifically to intimidate those unfortunate enough to stand in the dock. The situation was surreal enough as it was, ten Blackpool lads stood in the dock, next to eight Preston lads, all co-accused, and nearly as many barristers representing them. I stood there with my spiked hair that was spattered with bleach and crazy colour pink. I'd been advised to put my hands behind my back so the judge didn't see my tattoos, to look respectable for the court. We were in courtroom number one for our plea; it took nearly a morning to work out who was representing whom. This was the biggest courtroom they had, and the oak panelling stretched from the floor to the ceiling; oil paintings of judges wearing their grand robes and curly white wigs hung on the walls as a reminder of who was in control. Brass railings surrounded us, the dock was bursting at the seams, and the many prison officers were weighing up this new, unusual breed that was now in their custody. We entered our plea to the judge that day; mine was not guilty. Some months later, at my trial, I was found not guilty along with seven others. It's very difficult in a brawl such as this to prove who actually did what.

One thing about this whole affair that bothered me greatly was that a young man lay in the morgue dead. When I was questioned further about the incident a week later, the C.I.D. showed me a photo of this man lying on a slab with his head now shaved. It was clear to see the hole in his head, where the chair leg pierced the skull and entered his brain. I hadn't hit anyone with or thrown a chair, but I was as responsible as the next man who fought on that night. I desperately wished I could rewind the events of that evening and create a different outcome for this kid and his family, but that was never within my control; more drugs would soothe my conscience, and they did.

Chapter Eight

A few months had passed since the punk gig. I was sitting in a squat, in town, with a couple of friends trying to work out how to screw the chemist a few doors down the street. Danny and I laughed and rubbed our hands together because we'd sussed it out and were imagining all those beautiful drugs. If we broke into the flat next door, went halfway up the staircase, then took two stairs out, we could then drop into the pharmacy. All we'd have to do now was pick a night and get the job done. We decided on the Monday.

Sunday evening, Danny and I sat having a dig of barbs when three mates turned up at the door looking for drugs; we'd just finished our last. After some debate, we decided to throw caution to the wind and tackle the chemist there and then. Against our better judgment, we took them with us. This would never have been a consideration if we weren't stoned. So we walked into town, with our tools in a bag, and en route we passed two coppers stood in a shop doorway. "Evening, officer," said Danny before they had a chance to challenge us. The sarcasm in his voice brought a smirk to our faces. "Where you boys going?" We just kept walking, as though everything was cool. "We're off to our mates, to watch a film!" we shouted back, which seemed to satisfy their curiosity. About five minutes later, we arrived. We could see no lights in the upstairs flat, next door to the chemist, so we hung back for the passing cars to go by, their lights exposing our frames against the wall. The door went through with a resounding bang, and the staircase was before us. We'd estimated that if we took out the ninth and tenth step, we could drop straight into the pharmacy. I took the crowbar from the bag and started working on the steps. Once they were out, we peered through and saw shelving stacked neatly with canisters full of pills. What we hadn't taken into account, with our new grafting partners was who'd drop down and get the D.D.A. box. So a full-blown argument ensued, which made more noise than a dozen doors going through. This was now more like a pantomime than a burglary. Danny and I had the best case for one of them going through, as we'd let them in on our job. And now there was a striking chance of us getting our collars felt. We were relieved when Adam very reluctantly agreed to go down what I was now calling my hole. Davey, the older one of the three, who'd come with us, was now flapping, saying, "Come on, lads, let's fuck off; we'll get nicked for this."

"Shut up, ya prick; we're in now. It's too late for that. You shouldn't have come with us, but since you have, you're staying put!" Danny shouted at him. We held Adam's arms to support his weight as he prepared to drop down. "On the count of three, we'll let go, OK, Adam?"

"Yeah, man; let's get it done and get the fuck out of it. One, two, three." We expected to hear his feet touch the ground a few seconds later. "Aaargh!" Thud, a pile of boxes filled with nappies, broke his fall. "You bastards never said it was this high," came the muffled reply from the hole. At this point, we cracked up laughing. I dropped the crowbar down for him to get the box open and realized just how long the drop down was. "Fucking watch what you're doing, will ya? That just fucking hit me." The pharmacy staff used quite long ladders to get to the top shelves we could see. Adam was not a happy man. There was now no more time for any more dicking around. "Can you see the box, Adam?"

"Yeah, it's a big fucker," came the reply. We could hear Adam as he started to jimmy it off the wall. My thoughts turned to all the drugs inside when suddenly blue flashing lights lit up our faces from the street outside. "Adam, quick, put the ladders up and get out. The filth are here, come on, hurry up." Police cars now filled the street, sirens blasting out across the town centre. It was now every man for himself. We darted off in different directions; I ran to the flat upstairs, booted the door through and climbed out of the first-floor window. I ran along the shop roofs until I thought I was safe, then jumped down. I took off running, not looking back. As I turned the corner, I saw the police car driving towards me at speed. I turned quickly to see a copper was now chasing me on foot and was closing in on me. "Come here, Grimes, you little fucker." My head hit the ground as I was rugby tackled. No prizes for guessing this copper played a wicked game of rugby, so that was me nicked. When I arrived at the police station, I wondered if the others had got away. As we walked into the cells, I could hear Danny screaming. When he kicked off, he usually caused significant damage to whoever was in front of him. He was only five-foot-eight, but bulging with fifteen stones of pure muscle, a force to be reckoned with as he had more bottle than sense; he was fearless. I knew immediately this would be a lively stay in custody. Once I had reluctantly surrendered my clothes for forensics and put on a white paper boiler suit, I was taken to a room for questioning. They locked me in what I guessed was a medical room. About five minutes later, two large detectives walked in. They were dressed in dark suits and wouldn't have looked out of place carrying a coffin. I knew I was in for a hard time by the no-nonsense look on their faces. One of them walked over and introduced himself to me, put his hand on my shoulder and rapidly with his other hand, punched me hard in the stomach. I doubled over as I gasped for breath, winded. The other one grabbed my hair and straightened me up, and he punched me again in the stomach. This time, I dropped to the floor. I couldn't resist myself now, "You pair of wankers aren't real detectives, you need a brain for that. You can only beat up kids. Bet you'd shit yourselves if you were faced with a real criminal, wankers." The pain in my back made me arch backwards when I was kicked in the kidneys. One of the coppers walked over and thoughtfully picked up two medical books from the shelf, as thick as telephone directories. His huge hands were big enough to hold one in each hand. I remember wondering what he wanted with them. I soon found out, as he crashed them together on either side of my head, each time he asked me a question, as though they were a pair of symbols. My ears were ringing and burning. I could see his mouth moving but couldn't hear what he was saying.

I thought, *Fuck you, mate; you'll find nothing out from me, even if I could hear what you were drawling on about.* So the more the detective hit me with the books, I decided the best thing to do was laugh and stare directly at him; I don't know if that was the reaction he usually got, but he didn't do it again, and I didn't want to give them the pleasure of knowing how much it hurt me. When the ringing in my ears had stopped, the door swung open, and I was on my way to get my photo taken. Danny was just coming from having his mug-shots done. "Phil, what do they know? Fuck all from me mate, nothing. Did they get the others?" We heard voices from around the corner, then we saw Davey walking towards us in his underwear, with the two detectives who'd assaulted me minutes before. "You might as well tell 'em, lads. They know everything." Danny and I looked at each other; we'd just got a beating and said nowt, and he'd spewed his guts, first opportunity. We were later charged with burglary and banged in a cell until the next day when we'd face the magistrates in court.

In court the next day, Danny and I were remanded in custody for a week for psychiatric reports. There weren't many kids of our age breaking into pharmacies, so their first reaction was that we were mad.

Risley was a remand centre in Warrington, renowned for its violence and high rates of suicide, along with its nickname, Grisly Risley: it had a bad reputation.

I stood at one end of a long corridor with my bedroll under one arm, my pillowcase in the other, in my oversized prison issue brown denim clothing, which hung loosely from me. The wooden door was opened to reveal the strong bars of another gate. The smell was nothing short of sickening; it had all the fragrance of a hospital sluice multiplied by ten, sewage, body odour and tobacco smoke, with the heat from the pipes making the stench more intensive. This hospital, and I use that term loosely, was nothing short of a zoo. All along the ground floor were tiny cells. Opposite them were the strip cells, then further down the landing were the padded cells. All these prisoners could hear all day were the muffled cries that tried to penetrate the soundproof door. The only other source of stimulation they had was to watch other prisoners being dragged, kicking and screaming to their punishment. I glanced at a couple of the cards outside the doors, which carried a prisoner's details and sentence, life, fifteen years, HMP. I tried imagining what the massive black guy in the end pad was crying about and wondered how come he had a yellow strip down the front of his trousers. All these men had recently been either 'lifed-up' or given a big sentence and now awaited transfer to a local nick for allocation. I thought, *I might die in this place, or worst still, be raped and survive.* I was taken upstairs to the top floor which was made up of locked wards, twenty men on each. As the gate was unlocked, I soon noticed this was an adult prison with a handful of young men awaiting assessment, like myself thrown in. Nine of the men on my ward were awaiting trial for murder, two for arson, the other men were up on a variety of charges. One of the younger lads, who was twenty, had screwed a chemist; when I told him what my charge was, he was eager to know the details of what we'd got up to. I was shown to my bed, which were in rows; in the bed next to where I was to sleep was this bloke who'd strangled two people. I was determined to sleep with one eye open that night. I got talking to the Welsh lad, who like myself, was in for a chemist. He gave me the rundown on my new neighbours. "He killed his wife; he burned a house down, and that bloke there, chopped someone's hand off, killed them and dumped the body in a quarry."

There were two screws watching from a room, through glass, "This place is cushy, Phil, you'll get used to it." I had no intentions of being in there long enough to get used to it.

I couldn't wait to get my assessment over and done with, then I could go on the normal wing. I saw Danny out on exercise the next day, "We've got a visit today, Phil, my mum has rung the ward." I was now feeling rough and couldn't wait to see my parents. When I got back to the ward, I sat down to talk with Taffy; he told me he was on a visit and was getting some gear in and he'd turn me on, I couldn't wait. It was two o'clock when my name was called out for a visit. I walked through the gate to see Danny stood there beaming," They're here, Phil."

I sat in my cubicle behind two pieces of toughened glass; wire ran through the middle to strengthen it. When I looked at the mesh strip where you were supposed to talk through, I reflected to myself, *If, as the law states, you are supposedly innocent until proven guilty, I wouldn't like to see the visiting room for those who are convicted.* The room was badly lit, and the conversation of other prisoners shouting through the mesh to their loved ones became familiar background noise as my ears adjusted to the volume. That moment, my mum and dad appeared on the other side of the glass. A few moments later, my grandma walked slowly to join them. It was then that the enormity of the situation I now found myself in hit me face on. I gulped first, and then my eyes filled up. After a few seconds, I sobbed, "I'm sorry, I'm sorry. I won't do anything like this again, I promise. I'm never going to use drugs again, that's it. I'm going to get my life sorted out now, I promise." I felt devastated when I saw the look of hurt on their faces; they all cried too.

They were so out of place in the surroundings; I then felt guilty for them having to visit me in prison. It was then I said to myself, "Phil, you've got to get your shit together." I'd never looked at my drug taking in this light before, and I meant every word, at that moment, at that time. Momentarily, the veil was parted, and I could see that my actions were hurting others, and this felt terrible. I now knew I had a problem and was full of good intentions. I had a bigger problem, though, which was taking my good intentions and turning them into actions. I really believed my relationship with drugs had come to a definite end. Personal responsibility was a concept that was alien to me and my particular mindset. The solution, as far as I could see, was to get a good job, go to college, find a decent girlfriend. It didn't occur to me that I might be the problem.

Court soon came around, and we were back in front of the magistrate. I walked out of court with a hundred pound fine and two years' probation. Before I left the building, I visited the toilet and had a dig of Palfium, which someone brought to the court for me. All my good intentions were put on hold for the moment I flushed the opiates around my body; drugs again top of my agenda. I walked rubbing my now very itchy nose, out from the toilet straight into the path of my new probation officer. "Ah, Mr Grimes, we didn't get off to a flying start when you were on remand; maybe we could give it another go?"

Brian was your stereotypical social worker, from his Hush Puppy shoes to his tweed jacket with leather elbow patches. His long curly hair and scruffy beard made him look like he'd just bounced out of the student union; he was only missing a spliff. Brian wanted to see me in his office the next day, "And don't come stoned. I'm serious, Phil, I won't tolerate any messing about."

"Yeah, yeah, I'll be straight, Brian," I replied. He didn't appreciate the note of sarcasm in my voice. I had been told by Danny that he was fresh from university and wanted to make an impression.

Chapter Nine

The following day, I walked into his office where he was writing at a desk; it looked like it might break under the amount of paperwork piled up. Engulfed in a cloud of cigarette smoke, he puffed on a Marlboro. His back to me, he shouted, "Right, Phil, I've been looking at residential rehab for you but don't think you're ready as yet. But I have found a day project I'd like you to attend, where you can get some help!" I reluctantly agreed to this before he let me have his next line. "Oh, by the way, did I tell you it's in Manchester!" Two weeks later, I sat in his rusty old dolly tub Citroen, on my way through Blackpool, heading for Manchester. I desperately hoped none of my mates would see me in this poor excuse for a car and wondered if this heap would actually make the journey.

We arrived in Levenshulme just after lunch; he stopped the car abruptly outside this large house as if to make a point, "OK, Phil, we're here. I want you to give this your best shot. I've gone to a lot of trouble to sort this out for you." I sat there thinking, *Nice one, thanks so much, Bri.*

I felt totally manipulated and railroaded into sorting my life out and was feeling resentful because the whole thing happened so quickly, and I felt totally conned. "Thanks, Brian," I replied, with not an ounce of gratitude in my tone. The minute we pulled up outside the hostel which would be my home for the next few weeks, I felt panicky and anxious, as we waited in silence at the huge oak front door. The old couple who ran this place were amazing people, they were the warmest, most genuine people you could ever hope to meet. Hearts devoted one hundred per cent to the people in their care, and you could feel they weren't doing the job just for money. They instantly made me feel at home, made me a brew and introduced me to the other residents.

The following day, I had to attend 'Lifeline' in the city centre. I climbed the steps of this large terraced building and knocked at the big heavy door, hoping the staff might have walked out on strike or not turned up due to illness.

After two minutes and no reply, I turned to walk away, when the door swung open. This guy stood there who looked just like he had arrived back from Woodstock. "Wanna coffee man? Oh, my name's Rowdy Yates. Christine will be up in a minute, she's going to be your counsellor." I got my coffee and was led down to the basement. Rowdy opened the door as this woman walked from the room. Christine was a tall woman who looked like she knew the score and would take no shit.

"You'll be working in the woodwork room with a guy called Pete," she said... "On the hour, every hour, you'll come and talk with me, OK?" I was taken to another room in the basement and introduced to Pete. I recognized his face; he was from Wigan Casino, so we hit it off straight away. He was about twenty-four, with brown hair and a pale complexion. We sat in this bare room and laughed about how the staff had described it as their woodwork room. We were each given an old wooden table, the size of a small snooker table. Rowdy said, "I want you to sand this down to the wood."

At first, I thought he was joking, but there wasn't the slightest look of amusement on his face. I wondered how I'd allowed my probation officer to talk me into this. Rowdy was still stood looking at me with his piercing eyes, arms now folded in silence, and so I made a very resentful start at sanding my table.

After ten minutes, I thought I'd earned myself a break and stopped, when I heard a voice from the other side of the door shout, "Keep going, Phil, you can have a break at eleven!" I laughed, thinking, *How's this going to keep me clean*? I talked with my counsellor who told me I had a bad attitude. She said I needed to develop an attitude of gratitude towards the counselling at Lifeline; that our attitude determines one's altitude in life, how right she was, but her words went straight over my head. These people always seemed to have an endless supply of one-liners. I don't know if it was my age or that I wasn't desperate enough yet? I looked forward to our little chats, not least because she had a heater in her room, as we were freezing our bollocks off in the woodwork room. After a few days of sanding, Pete and I were growing weary of the woodwork. I'd agreed to go with him to his mum's, so we took the bus to Stockport. As we walked up to his mum's place, I realized Pete and his mum lived in the flat belonging to a post office, and she was the postmistress.

We sat down at the table, and I thanked his mum for the offer of egg and chips. His mum went back into the kitchen. Pete jumped up and tiptoed across the room towards a hook on the opposite wall with a large bunch of keys hanging from it. He motioned to me with his finger on his lips, and as he disappeared through the door into the actual post office, I shook my head thinking, *This is bang on-top. He's gonna get well and truly rumbled here.* Pete's mother walked back into the room with my plate of food, saying, "Where's our Peter?"

"He's gone to the toilet, Mrs. A"

I was well relieved when she went back into the kitchen.

Moments later, she was back with Pete's dinner. "Where is the li'l . . . ?" This was a rhetorical question, as she suddenly turned and made for the door Pete had disappeared through. At that same moment, Pete was on his way back through the same door when they bumped right into each other. There was a strange silence for a couple of seconds. Pete had hundreds of pounds scooped up in his jumper which went up in the air. I sat there with my jaw wide open, not knowing whether to laugh or cry. The twenty-pound notes were floating to the ground, almost in slow motion, as they rested on the floor. "Right, I'm calling the police this time, Peter!" shouted his mum, as she ran out the back door.

Pete picked up the money from the floor. I was still sat there with my mouth open, about to put a fork full of chips into my mouth. I threw my knife and fork down, and we legged it out the back. We ran down the road. "You really fucked things up, Pete, you wanker!" I screamed at him. I could almost hear prison doors slamming behind me. "She won't do anything, Phil."

"I don't care; that was too heavy."

We ran for another five minutes and stopped outside a working men's club. "Let's get a drink, Pete, so we can think what we're going to do next." We sat in the labour club for half an hour waiting for his dealer to arrive; scored some heroin and went back to the hostel. In my room, we counted twelve hundred pounds each. That night, I wondered if we'd get our collars felt at Lifeline the next day. I stuffed my half in a sock, had a hit, and worried no more.

I was amazed that the next day nothing was said to either of us about the incident. But later in the day, I was pulled into the office as one of the staff had clocked my eyes and asked me how come they were pinned. I was asked to leave. I jumped on the train back to Blackpool and was at a friend's flat, having a dig, within ten minutes of my arrival home.

Days after getting back, I'd started back at the circus for another season. I knew this would sort of hold me together because I had to be relatively clear during the show, and there were two shows a day. However, I was truly back on the hamster's wheel. A friend had given me the number of two private doctors who would script me up for anything I wanted. It sounded almost too good to be true. One of these doctors was an alcoholic and was happy to be paid with a bottle of whisky. Dr Davis was an old guy who simply asked me when I walked in, "What do you want, son?" If I wanted Durophet, Dexedrine, Nembutal, "Or is it something else you needed?" he'd ask.

Seeing he was asking, I thought might as well go for a full house. He wrote me up for Nembutal, Durophet, and Diconal on separate scripts. I handed over the bottle of whisky and a tenner, and as I'd got an extra item on my script, I was very happy. Later in the week, I went to my next appointment with Dr Harris and got the same from him. I looked at blagging doctors as a challenge, and lying to them was second nature to me now; some of the time, I got a result, and there were many occasions when I didn't, but now I had three definite suppliers.

Chapter Ten

One winter's day, I stayed at this couple's house, Pete and Lynda.

They were easily ten years older than I was. She was a thoroughly decent person, and I enjoyed talking to her; he wasn't such a nice person, and he bullied Lynda verbally and put her down, and I didn't fully trust him. When he brought his drugs out, which was rare, he was one of those people who never let you forget it, quite a tight-arse really, and he'd expect something in return. This night he was overly generous, which got me thinking what's he after? He started to tell me about his ex-pad mate he'd been in jail with, and with whom he'd had a fight. This was someone I knew and got on with, John. I'd been out with John a few nights previously. He was speeding off his head; last thing I heard was when he got home he got it into his head he'd caught crabs so shaved every bit of hair from his body, head too.

I hadn't seen him since that night, but rumour was he looked a treat. There was something about this night which I couldn't put my finger on; there was a weird atmosphere, but I put it down to me being over-sensitive. Lynda brought a sleeping bag downstairs as it had got quite late. I'd decided to get my head down on the couch. Pete, Lynda, and their two kids had gone upstairs to bed. This other guy, who I hadn't met before, was staying over too. That's how it was; it was a very open house. I fell into a light sleep, which was unusual for me, as I can sleep on a washing line, but I still had that uneasy feeling I'd experienced earlier. I must have drifted into a deeper sleep, when after about an hour, bang, bang, bang. I sat up as I heard the back door go in. My first thought was that we were getting busted by the drug squad. For some reason, I lay back down on the couch thinking, *Fuck off and leave me alone.*

The lounge door opened quickly; the lights blinded me momentarily, and as I focused my eyes, five faces were looking down at me. "Hey, Phil, what the fuck are you doing here?" I knew why I'd been feeling uneasy.

"I've just crashed down here for the night, what the fuck are you doing here, more like?" and we all laughed at what was now a weird situation. John was now looking extremely agitated, "Listen, Phil, I've come to sort things out with that miserable twat upstairs; will you go and let him know I'm here?" said John.

"Half the street must have heard you put the door through, including Pete, but yeah, I won't be a minute; let me get out of this sleeping bag," I replied.

I walked into Pete's bedroom, and he'd worked out what was going on. He pulled his jeans on, reached over to the bedside cabinet and slid a knife into his back pocket.

When Pete and John's eyes met they ran at each other with their heads down. There was a dull thud as skull smashed against skull, like buffalo locking horns; everyone else backed away. Pete reached into his back pocket and stuck John in the chest; the squelching sound signalled it was all over. John walked into the back of the ambulance, laid down and died. At that moment, I hit the deck and remember coming round in the interview room at Blackpool Central, with a piercing headache second to none. I felt my head where I found a huge lump that was sticky with congealed blood. Two detectives entered the room; one walked straight towards where I sat and knocked my feet off the table. "Right, this is a murder inquiry; how did you get those injuries to your head?" I walked from the police station after barely minimal co-operation, wondering, *What the fuck is all this about? John is lying in the morgue.* I'd had a drug-induced fit and was really spaced out. I needed to get to score and sort my head out, and that took a matter of half an hour, then everything was OK again. The horror of the previous night melted into my unconscious mind. I was no stranger to death now. Two people I knew were now dead from drug overdoses. This had directed my thoughts inwards, and I made an inner vow to myself to not get close to anyone. It was my protection plan against pain, so I built walls around myself; I was already what could be considered a loner and had been for some years. I had lots of mates and knew lots of people, but even in a crowd, I could feel alone. I didn't seem to be able to work it out; how come these invisible barriers existed? I'd crossed a bridge somewhere along the road.

A week later, I lay in the A&E department again. I could clearly see myself lying on a hospital bed now, as I left my body. I walked around the back of the doctors who were working on my physical shell and watched as the crash team put these electrodes on my chest and my back arched under the power of the current.

I stood and watched with some curiosity at the concern on the faces of the doctors and nurses. I enjoyed being out of my body. I looked at the clock; it was five past six. I saw a taxi pull up outside under the window. I don't really know what prompted me, exactly, but I just knew it was time to go back and re-join myself.

The hospital staff still shot electric currents into me. I walked around the back of them, as they faced me on the table, and climbed back into myself.

Later on, I told one of the nurses about my experience; they reassured me it was not unusual, and there was someone on their way over to discuss it with me. I was now starting to regret saying anything. I asked the psychologist at what time did my heart stop beating? "Five past six precisely," he replied. I left the hospital still out of my head but still thoughtful about my out-of-body experience.

I tried to put events in the hospital to the back of my mind, so I went to the pub with a friend. We had no money, so we decided to go into town to see if we could rob a one-armed bandit and see if anything was happening down at the snooker hall. En route, we called into the amusement arcade. We heard someone whistle, then saw a couple of mates waving us over. They were getting some grief from these blokes playing a machine in the corner. Next thing I knew it was off, feet and fists were flying everywhere, screaming and shouting echoed around the place, over the top of the computerized noise from the slot machines. I saw a flash of something in the corner of my eye, then someone who stood to my left slammed a metal bin into the side of my head which knocked me to the ground.

I curled into a ball because I knew what was coming, I felt two or three boots sink into my back; believe me, they hurt more than getting hit with the bin. The kicks stopped which I thought strange, then I reasoned with myself to deal with the pain later. I leapt up, grabbed this guy who was hitting my pal in the face, and I rammed his head into the pinball machine a few times. When I looked up to see loads of coppers piling through the door, I ran over to the other side of the arcade, out through the fire exit and down the street with two coppers chasing after me. I had put a healthy distance between me and the coppers, so I walked into a department store and walked out another door onto a different street, only yards away from the snooker hall. I flew down the stairs of the snooker hall and walked in as though not in a rush. This was a massive basement area that was pitch dark; the only light coming from above the tables. I walked to the far side of the hall so that if anyone came in, I could dive behind one of the drapes which hung over the outer wall of the place.

After half an hour had gone by, I decided to leave, thinking everything would have blown over and walked straight into the arms of the police. I appeared in court, and my case was adjourned for a couple of months for reports and stuff.

I was due in court a couple of months later. The night before court, my mum decided I would look much better if she bleached the different colours out of my hair. When she had finished, my hair was brilliant white with a pink stripe down the middle. I thought it looked brilliant, but not quite what you want when you're wanting to blend in with the crowd. I went to court in my friend's blue suit, which clashed massively with my hair. I saw the magistrate do a double take when he clapped eyes on me, and I knew my new look had done me no favours whatsoever. I was sent to a detention centre.

When I got out of DC, I pumped every drug I could get my hands on into my arm, with a desperation that wasn't really rational. I was in full self-destruct mode; I often said to myself, "I don't give a fuck; why should I care?"

Everywhere I went, I carried a knife. I didn't care for myself, so why should I care about anyone else? I was out most nights burgling houses, shops, warehouses, and a couple of chemists, and I slept where I landed. I was in and out of hospital, overdosed just about every week. I re-established my relationship with my private doctors and was scoring gear off the street when there were no decent pharmaceuticals about. When I woke in the morning, I'd pull back my curtains, and it didn't matter if the sun was beating down or the birds were singing, to me every day was overcast. The only thing that mattered to me now was my drugs, they sustained me and had become part of my DNA, permeating my every cell and making music with my central nervous system. They took me on the wildest journeys, where no one else could follow, deep inside my own neurology. Being straight was hell on earth like fingernails scraping down a blackboard. When I didn't have them, my head was a battlefield, one where I fought and lost against the Devil and his demons. There were only one winner and one loser; I just couldn't find it in me to admit defeat.

Chapter Eleven

I was in Jenks bar, in the town centre and stumbled across this guy at the bar who said he'd pay me well if I could get him some black bombers. Not a problem, as my script was due. I arranged to meet him at his work. I turned up as arranged to this little tobacconist shop, tucked away in the town centre and waited until his last customers had left.

I gave him what I'd brought along, I thought twenty was plenty, as I didn't know him and was paranoid he might be setting me up. He was a public schoolboy, who talked with a plum in his mouth, so I was thinking, who is this guy?

When it came to handing over money, he asked me what he owed me, so fooling around, I said, "That's two hundred quid, mate." I thought my horses had all come in at once when he stuck it in my hand and thanked me.

Before I left, I said to him, "Stick with me, and I'll look after you." I was desperately trying not to laugh; I would have charged anyone else twenty. He shouted down the street, "Call back on Friday!" I crossed the street and walked into the pub to celebrate. This was the beginning of the eighties, and I had got involved with a team of pickpockets who were active in the town. I was absolutely rubbish and by far too clumsy to relieve someone of their wallet, but these guys were really good. So I became the decoy for a while because they were making a lot of money, and I thought *why not*.

There were easy pickings at the Pleasure Beach, and it paid a good wage. We would wait around the bus stop or the taxi rank for holidaymakers to arrive on the bus. Once we spotted the mark, we'd sandwich them between two of us. The one in front would stall so the mark would walk into the back of them, then the person behind would bump them, dipping into their pocket whilst another team member would be passing at that moment and take the wallet. When business wasn't good, we'd go to the nearest pub, and one of us would go to the bar; the other two would stand back and observe. The one at the bar would shout, "Some bastard has stolen my wallet!" When the rest of those around the bar heard this, their hands would go straight onto the pocket containing their valuables to check they still had theirs. So now we knew exactly which pockets to hit. We'd wait and watch, let them have a few more drinks, then relieve them of their valuables by bumping them on the way to the toilet, sometimes even at the bar. The cheekier you are, the better it works. There were always rich pickings in Blackpool, especially in the clubs. We'd go to the Mecca, a club with a massive dance floor, find a group of women busy dancing around their handbags and start dancing with them. One of us would cause a distraction by kicking a bag to the side, and one us would be waiting to pick it up. It was then thrown to the third person, standing near the toilet. He'd take it in the bogs and empty it. It was a means to an end for me so I could buy my drugs.

Holidaymakers were fair game, but I knew it wouldn't last forever, as I needed drugs in me to keep me together to pull it off.

One night, we were doing our usual caper at the Mecca when this bloke clocked us doing a bag; it happened to be his girlfriend's. He was a huge miner, from Barnsley; the only thing I remember seeing before he knocked me clean out was this big tattooed fist. Then the others dived in and rescued me as now he was kicking me round like a rag doll. Before we left the club, we teamed up with the rest of the Blackpool lads. There were always running battles when the place shut. The guy who nearly punched my head off my shoulders was waiting for me, with the rest of his coach party. I walked over to him, signalling for him to come over to me. "Look, mate, there's something you need to know before it kicks off." I couldn't believe my luck when he leaned forward, "Fuck off, yer thieving bastard," he said. I knew this caveman would snap me in two, so not being one for the Queensberry Rules, I butted him hard on his temple, and he dropped to the floor, and I kicked him in the head until he made no more noise. It was him or me. I thought, *There has got to be an easier way to earn a living.*

Every day I woke and saw daylight; I knew I had to graft. I thought I'd go and see Billy at the tobacconist and see if he wanted any more drugs. "Where have you been, Phil, I've been trying to get hold of you?" I sold him more speed at the same price. I thought, *If he's daft enough to pay this price, he must have more money than sense.*

I'm sat in a pub in the town, with a few mates one day and Billy walked in, "Hi, Phil, how are you?" he said. Everyone turned their heads when they heard Billy's public schoolboy accent. I thought it best to talk with him outside before he dropped himself in it. He seemed really out of place in this boozer. I leaned against the wall, "Look Billy, don't start talking about drugs in front of people you don't know, and by the way, don't be flashing money around like it's going out of fashion." I could see he was bursting to tell me something, "Phil, I'm having a party on Saturday, can you get me some speed and acid?" So we arranged to meet, and I took him his drugs. My own drug habit was escalating, and my behaviour was more than chaotic. I was busted for possession of Class A drugs and theft, which meant spending some more time in Risley, on remand. Whilst on remand, I reflected on how meaningless life had become, and now realized that I had to make some changes in my life but didn't have a clue where to start. I'd once said to my dad when talking about my drug problem that if it weren't for the doctors, I wouldn't have a drug problem, and I'd been dealt a duff hand. He said, "Phil, it's how you play your hand that counts, not what cards you get. A good card player can do a lot with a duff hand." I loved this man dearly. He didn't say a lot, but when he did, he knew what he was on about. I needed a different game to play, but unless I knew where to find it, I'd have to stick with this one.

My sentence was deferred at court, so if I kept my nose clean, I'd be OK. It was good just to be back on the street. I'd been home a couple of days when my mum came home from work to find me overdosed in my bedroom. I'd injected some Nembutal and took the knock. I only remember coming around in hospital and hearing my mum's voice in the distance. We drove home in silence until Mum started to cry, "I've had enough, Phil; it's got to stop now, or I'll do something about it, 'cause I can't go on like this." And at that point, she started to drive at a tree. I grabbed the wheel, and we straightened up again "OK, Mum, I'll go see my probation officer and see if I can get myself in a rehab. Or maybe a decent job will do it," I said.

I saw Billy again in his shop; he said he was leaving off the speed for a while. He'd told me he didn't want his dad to find out what he was doing, but there was something else I might be able to help him out with. "I've been getting some hassle off these lads coming in the shop," he said. "Not a problem, Billy, I'll get it sorted," I replied. I knew the lads concerned quite well; in fact, I drank with one of them. All that happened was I had a few drinks with them and asked them to leave it out, and that was that. When I told Billy it was over, he pushed three hundred pounds into my pocket, just for talking to someone. A few days later, I arranged for a couple of lads to go in and cause a bit of trouble. I turned up at the shop shortly afterwards. It was clear they'd caused him some concern, so that was another three hundred quid. And on this went for quite some time, as well as the ridiculous prices for his speed, I took 'grands'. Billy's common sense was nowhere near on a par with his intellect; he was a clever guy, really, but his need to prove to his father that he had his business and personal life under control was greater. His extremely rich parents gave him more or less what he wanted. As time went on, I had to come up with another blag, so I told him I had two lock-ups full of bent cigarettes, and he bought it. He'd paid for them three times over.

I was nicked again, this time for carrying a knife, so I was in breach of the deferred sentence.

I thought I could use this to get into rehab. My probation officer made the arrangements, so now it was a condition of my probation that I went there. I stood at the door of Inward House, in Lancaster, with my suitcase in my hand. I had been drug-free for twenty-four hours now and wondered if I'd suffered some sort of mental health disorder that had made rehab sound like a good idea. My mouth was so dry, it felt like sandpaper. I was pouring with sweat, yet shivering, and my nose was streaming when the door opened. "Hi, you must be Phil? I'm Peter." Once I'd finished some paperwork, I was led towards the lounge area to meet everyone. The door opened, and I peered into a darkened room, lit only by candles, to see a group of twelve men lying on the carpet, holding hands and gazing at the ceiling, listening to a Lenard Cohen track, with their eyes closed. "What is all this about?" I said. I needed the toilet and left them to surf the cosmic plains. I sat on the loo thinking, *I've made a massive mistake to put myself up for this.*

I slept in a room with a mate of mine from Blackpool. He'd been there for nine months and was about to graduate. He didn't appear to be the same guy to me, far more introverted than usual; he'd lost the glint in his eye, and all he talked about was the programme.

He left a week later to move into his flat. Three days later, we were told that Paul was now dead. He'd robbed a nearby chemist, got arrested, and hung himself on a bandage in the police cells. I said to myself, "If this is rehab, you can keep it." I received a cheque by post; a member of staff walked with me to the bank. I cashed the cheque, waved goodbye to the staff, and jumped into a waiting taxi. I phoned my probation officer before I caught the train. He told me how I was now in breach of my order and would be picked up by the police eventually. I felt angry and resentful towards my probation officer, as my going to rehab was my idea, not his, not the courts, and now he'd dropped me right in it, although he was only doing his job.

I'd been back a couple of days and spent my time wasted in the pub. I'd been in to see Billy at the shop, and I asked him if he could give me a couple of hundred up front and I'd bring him some speed in the following day. "Can't do it, Phil. Dad's onto me, I'm easing off a bit," he said. "It doesn't work like that Billy; I want some fucking money out the till, now."

I was too drunk to hear the two people who walked in behind. I picked up the weighing scales from the counter when I heard a radio crackle. I threw the scales, spun around and ran from the shop as a police car mounted the pavement and accelerated towards me. It was just as well I jumped to the side, or it would have been back to the hospital. Another car stopped in the middle of Talbot Road and blocked my only escape route, I was grabbed from behind. Game over.

I was back in the dock at Preston Crown Court. I stood in front of Judge Locket, otherwise known as Last Chance Locket. He gave me nine months imprisonment, although I'd already done two months on remand. So with four months left to do, I could be out for Christmas if everything went well and I lost no days.

Walton Prison, Liverpool, another huge Victorian institution with a dark, oppressive presence. I walked along the landing with its wall-to-wall rabbit warrens. Some men were two and three to a cell, banged up for twenty-three hours a day. I was one of the cons now. I stood on A wing, outside the canteen looking down the main body of the jail, watching as the place was unlocked for exercise. I could spot a few mates which made me feel better. I got in single file and went with the flow of human traffic. Exercise was an hour a day, which was circles inside circles. The outer circle walked clockwise, then the next circle went anticlockwise, then one inside that one clockwise, and so on until those in the middle were chasing their tails. It was almost like watching the mechanism of a clock; the dark brickwork of the prison wing on each side cast its shadow over the yard. And as I thought about us in our blue and white striped shirts and blue jeans, it reminded me of something like you'd read in Dickens' books. We belonged to another place in time. There were fear and resentment mixed with mistrust and violence in the eyes of most men. I had worn a front for so many years, so adopting another one was no big deal to me. This wasn't a place where you could let anyone see your weaknesses — both screws and cons. Most of those I'd met up to now had given me the impression they took it all in their stride, but I knew in reality lots of men showed another face when behind their doors. I was put on I wing; this was the biggest wing in the nick. Everyone on I wing was unemployed, so it was pure bang up. I'd been put into a double cell. I didn't have a pad mate as yet but was expecting someone after tea. I could handle being in a cell on my own. I only had twelve weeks left to serve. I'd done twelve on remand, so I was out on the twenty-second of December.

Around four o'clock, the cell door was opened, and this guy walked in with his kit and belongings in a box. He was in his late thirties, I guessed, with brown-red hair and the look of a boxer about him. "Alright, my name's Brian," he said in a broad scouse accent. I introduced myself, and we sat down to smoke a spliff. He was doing a short sentence also, six months and had further charges to face. This man had educated himself and was defending himself in his pending court appearances. The box he carried with him was full of law books. Brian would talk for hours about his past exploits and have me howling with laughter. I didn't care if his stories were true or not. "Hey Phil, did I ever tell you about the time I sold a snide Rolex to an African warlord in Lagos and found myself in front of a firing squad?"

"No, Brian, you didn't, but I'm sure you're going to." This man was a very well respected and successful old-school villain, who made a lot of money at what he did, and I'm sure he could have carved out a career as a successful comedian or after dinner speaker; a top bloke.

I got on with my sentence and spent my exercise walking around with Stuart. He was much older than me and knew a lot of scams. He gave me all the details on how to defraud the post office, by entering money into savings books, then taking it out. As we walked in circles, we talked about all the chemists and doctors we'd screw on our release; this was what I focused on while being banged up.

I waited in my pad for my discharge board. This was where I had the chance to see if my clothes still fitted me. I'd lost weight over my time in custody. This was more to do with the prison's strict crimes against food policy. I'd never seen white cabbage before I came to Walton nick and the cheese wack we ate for breakfast needed a stomach made of cast iron to digest. After all, whoever ate corned beef, cheese, and potatoes all fried up in grease in the morning?

I was listening to John Lennon, "Happy Christmas War is Over" on the radio when a large over-sized pigeon landed on the window ledge wearing a tiny Liverpool scarf. It's amazing what a man would do to occupy himself when locked up. I took my clothes from the cardboard box they'd been in and put them on, they smelled musty, but it felt comforting to feel them against my skin again. My trousers hung from me, but I didn't care. I was going home! The twenty-second of December came soon enough. I said goodbye to my mates who were in for Christmas and shared the few belongings I'd accumulated and took a few messages for their families. One of the screws from my landing shouted me over, "Come on Grimes, you're going home, son, and stay off them silly fucking drugs!" I walked from the reception to the gate, and the cold air now seemed to feel better in my lungs. Everywhere had been covered with a dusting of snow, taking some of the harshness from the architecture. When I stood dwarfed by the big gates, I reflected over my time in prison and wondered what kind of society kept men in these conditions in the name of justice, then I was gone.

I sat down in front of my probation officer, expecting a lecture, so I'd switched off. He was going on and on as my eyes were fixed on looking at a crack in the ceiling. And to end his sermon, he asked me, "So what you going to do when you leave this office?"

I didn't have a doctor, and my head was full of schemes of how to acquire some drugs. "Oh, I'll probably leave here and hold a doctor up at knifepoint," I replied, sarcastically. "Oh right, oh right, let me make a phone call," he said and left the room. I immediately regretted even going to see him. When he returned, he shoved a piece of paper towards me. "I have got you on a doctor's list, and you need to call down there to pick up your script." I thought he was winding me up. "No Phil, I'm serious, get down there; I got someone else on this doctor's list last week."

The surgery was on my way home, so I popped in and spoke with the receptionist. I only gave her my name, and she handed me an envelope and said I'd have to call in daily to collect my script. I opened the envelope and saw four Diconal, two Nembutal, and two black bombers. My eyes were out on stalks. I hadn't even seen the doctor! I left the surgery and called at my friend's caravan, got my hit together, and realized what it was about drugs that I loved so much: they delivered.

Chapter Twelve

The doctor who I'd been put onto by my probation officer was bent, and it was a matter of eight weeks before I was collecting twenty-five Diconal each day, along with the two bombers, and two nembies. Nine months had gone by, and there was now no need for me to go out grafting with my doctor supplying my drugs, and it wasn't too long before life got really boring.

Most of my veins had now collapsed, and I was injecting into my groin. Instead of stabbing away at my arms, neck, legs, and feet I had access to what I thought would be a never-ending injection site. All I needed was a decent works and a sharp green spike. I was already hung up on hygiene when having a crank and had adopted a ritual which was becoming like preparing for a medical procedure. But once I'd had my hit, it made no difference whatsoever. I had woken up on the floor, with a works sticking out my groin, often in the dirtiest of places.

I weighed about nine stone, my skin had a deathly pale jaundiced glow. The circles under my eyes made them look like they were deeper set than usual. Any health, family, social, or even criminal consequences were light years away from my conscious thoughts.

I was arrogant and proud enough to think I'd either walk away from my drug taking, scot-free, when I was ready, or at worst die young of an overdose. The comment I became used to hearing that troubled me most was when friends and family would say, "Phil, you've changed; you've lost that glint in your eyes."

I made my usual trip to the doctor this particular day and asked the receptionist for my script. It was a different woman behind the desk, "Sorry Mr Grimes, Doctor has told me he can't see you anymore," she said. *What was she talking about?* I thought. She pushed a script towards me for some methadone amps, a week's worth. "That's your last."

I demanded to see the doctor there and then. "He's out doing house calls, Mr Grimes," she replied. Before I could say another word, I felt a hand on my shoulder and didn't need to turn around. I knew who it was immediately. I walked to the police car as I thought I'll call back when someone else was at reception.

I walked towards the psychiatric ward, down a long corridor, carrying my suitcase, as my footsteps echoed around me, wondering if this was the end of the line for me. I had friends who'd done their rattle in these places and still carried the mental scars.

So I took my seat in a waiting area outside the ward, which said, Acute Psychiatric.

The unit had only been opened a day, and I could still smell gloss paint. A woman came and sat in the chair next to me. She was drop-dead gorgeous, wearing a white blouse and black leather trousers, long dark hair tied back and quite a bonny face. She had her suitcase with her also. A guy popped his head around the corner to say someone would be along soon. I wondered if he was staff or a patient? She told me she hadn't waited long to be admitted, and at the moment she talked, she popped one of her breasts out and started to squeeze milk from her nipple. *Oh great*, I thought, *she's going to get me bunged out before I even started.* I imagined the psychiatrist's words to me, *"You've only been here five minutes, and you're leading the patients astray."* Minutes later, a female nurse appeared and simply said, "Carol, I think you might be embarrassing the young man," and they both disappeared into a room.

I sat down in front of the psychiatrist who made it plain from the word go he wasn't happy about having a junkie on his ward. I made it clear to him that this was a last resort for me too. He went on to inform me, in a manner like I was already on my final warning, that "We treat people here with real mental health problems, so be warned: any messing about, and you'll be gone. Oh, and by the way, I've written you up for Methadone, Heminevrin, Tuinal, and Largactil." I didn't have a clue what Largactil and Heminevrin were but knew this wasn't the time to ask. I spent the rest of the day and that evening in the TV room, where there was a nurse at all times. At nine o'clock, we were called for medication. I was nearly crushed under foot; this made the January sales look tame, as chairs were overturned and arguments started over who was first. Some of these people were not for reasoning with, so I waited until the maddening crowds had stilled and got mine last. My ward was closest to the office, and I was quite pleased about this.

I didn't really want to wake up and wished the person shaking me would go away. I opened my eyes to see an emaciated face, about an inch from mine. He was opening his mouth wide and then closing it, just as though he was a goldfish. His eyes bulged with madness, and his breath smelled like the pit of hell. Someone to my right shouted over, "Its only Andrew, he probably wants a fag!" I reached over to my locker, got my cigarettes, and he backed off, so I threw him a fag. His face changed from serious and strained to one of total joy and happiness with a smoke. I said, "Andrew, you can have a fag from me any time you want mate, but you ever wake me up and freak me out like that again, and we'll fall out; you understand me, Andrew?" He nodded his head in reply, not a man of many words.

The Methadone they gave me wasn't holding me together, but the other medication I was given had knocked me sideways, as I staggered towards the medication trolley. I told the nurse I was strung out and needed more Meth; she reassured me that it would be done later that morning. My days in the cuckoo's nest were long but never boring. Andrew, who was tormented with paranoid schizophrenia had a friend called John, who I enjoyed playing chess with. John had dropped some acid at a party, and he never found his way back home. His hair was long, and he would pace the ward in bare feet, calling for all to repent for the kingdom was at hand; yet he was a great chess player and a super intelligent man.

It really saddened me when I realized there was no way back to reality for John, as he found himself now trapped inside a terrifying world of demons, demons of the worst kind, which gave him no rest. At one point, he thought I was controlling him with my hand movements, then I could read his mind by telepathy. If I could, I'd get him to move his queen so that I could take it, but this wasn't the case.

The reality was even more cruel: psychiatric wards and strong medication were now his life, or maybe suicide if it all got too much. The staff in the nest were every bit as bonkers as the patients and played twisted games for their own amusement. I could see some of the victims who'd run foul of them, and I wasn't going to be another one. I was going out with one of the nurses from the medical ward at the time, so when she learned of my detox, she nipped over on her break. I had rehearsed what I would say to Carol. "Please, for fuck sake, Carol, you've got to sneak me out to the pub; this is doing my head in now. I need a break from it all." That afternoon, we sneaked off to the pub whilst staff thought I was sleeping. We sneaked back into the ward unnoticed, as the staff sat in the office and read their papers. My rattle had been fierce, so I spent many days and nights sat up in the quiet room with my bedcover draped over me shivering, smoking, and rubbing my aching bones, whilst trying to put reason and meaning to the crazy thoughts. I was convinced that I was no longer in an NHS psychiatric ward, but now it had become a government experiment, and the drugs I was being given were definitely not what they told me they were. I became mentally worn out, as I wouldn't eat the food as it was spiked, and now I'd started to wonder if the nurses really were nurses; it was time for me to leave. Carol came to see me again the following day, so at our first opportunity, we jibbed off to her place. Her flat appeared more luxurious than usual, the couch more comfortable, the colours of the painting on the wall hypnotized me; everything in the hospital staved my senses. I ate my fry-up Carol made and was happily sat there, swigging a can of lager.

It was time to return to the hospital for visiting. My mum and dad were coming to see me. Once I'd shown my face to the nurses, we went down to the front entrance where we stood smoking. Mum and Dad arrived; I gave them a hug and suggested we finish our cigs before we went in. My dad pointed out we shouldn't really be smoking with the fire censors above our heads. "Oh, it's OK, Dad; we stand here smoking all the time," I said. And to demonstrate my point I blew a cloud of smoke towards one. The sound of the smoke alarm was deafening. "Quick, let's hide in the car," Mum said. So we darted off towards the car park, when I realized my Dad was still standing there trying to look all innocent. I ran back and got him by the arm.

We all crouched down inside the car and watched whilst the nurses started to evacuate patients. I looked on at the scene of total chaos, as the nurses tried to coordinate those who were delusional and psychotic into groups so they could do a count. The old lady with multiple personality disorder pulled her long frock over her head like she did on the ward, to greet the doctor, revealing she wasn't wearing anything underneath, and visitors looked on in horror. That was when it dawned on me that I was in trouble. I was the only one who couldn't be accounted for. "You've bloody done it this time our Phillip," said my mum from the front of the car. I walked back onto the ward and saw my bag packed on top of my bed, so I knew it was on top. The nurse in charge walked up to me and asked if I would do a sample. I knew it was pointless because I'd drunk a can of lager earlier; I refused and was asked to leave.

Chapter Thirteen

I wasn't sorry to see the back of that place and would be happy when the whole experience was carefully tucked away in the basement of my mind so I could forget that my third attempt to get clean had indeed failed.

Time was now slipping through my fingers, as I looked out into the future. I had started to become depressed, thinking there's no way I'd ever get any kind of peace in my life. There was no real purpose to my life now that crime, hunting for drugs, then getting off my face had taken over, I felt like it would swallow me alive.

The lying, manipulating, ripping people off was getting to me now. When I looked around at others, it was as if they had it all sussed. Everyone appeared to know what they wanted, where they were going, and how to get there. Me, I was just lost, with no direction so put all my energies into drifting aimlessly from one hit to the next. I overdosed a few more times, as now, all I wanted to do was to shut down and tune out. I had been around Alex's place for a few days, and it had been a hell of a week. On day two, his little girl, Michelle, came running into the house crying. She'd been abused by this bloke who lived two doors down the street. I saw him coming home thinking the dust had settled and shouted to Alex and his wife, Julie. We flew out the house, just as the police arrived to nick him. I went to punch him, and a copper grabbed me. "You touch him, Grimes, and yer nicked." The nonce was laughing at me as if to say, "You can't touch me, I'm protected from the likes of you." A few hours later, he was out on bail. Three days later, we were sat in the house waiting to score when there was a tap at the door. Alex got up slowly as if wary of who was calling. It was only seven-thirty, and this dealer was never on time.

No sooner had he undone the latch when the door burst open, and Debbie ran into the hallway screaming and sobbing hysterically. We brought her into the living room and tried calming her down so that we could find out what had happened to her. Debs had experienced a lot of grief in her life, but I'd never seen her lose it like this. Her husband had died from an OD, her daughter taken by the social services, and in the last six months, she had lost her arm from injecting. Whatever had happened must have been bad! "He raped me, the bastard raped me!" Debbie screamed. We all looked at each other with wide eyes, and at first, a look of shock. Debbie continued to sob. As the shock wore off, I felt an anger and rage surge through me, "Whichever horrible twat has done this to her will pay dearly for it." It had only been days before when little Michelle had been touched by the nonce case from down the street. Now we learned that the man who'd done this was also someone who had previous sex offences against children; they seemed to be everywhere. Julie consoled Debs, whilst Alex and I plotted our revenge.

Half an hour later, when things had calmed down, we all decided to pay this guy a visit. We routed out three balaclavas, some rope, and a gun. We dropped some downers, then set off to get some justice of our own. Alex, Julie, and I waited around the corner. We'd decided to send Debs to the door, knowing he'd open it for her. The door creaked as it slowly opened up. We could only hear him trying to blag Debs by telling her how much he wanted her again. We heard enough; we put our ballys on and flew around the corner.

Debs had a pair of pliers in her hand when she backhanded him across the mouth. The crunch of broken teeth was audible, and they dropped from his mouth like broken porcelain.

He stood there crying and moaning in his shorts as we pushed him back into his living room. Alex offered himself as the ropes person, pushed him to the floor, and he hog-tied him so he couldn't move. Now it was time to let Debs have her say to her rapist, not a luxury most women get. She shouted, screamed, and cried. "You fucking animal, why, why, why?" she said gasping for breath as she sobbed. On a shelf stood a photo of her rapist with his arm around a small child. Debs held it above her head, then threw it at the wall. She took a long piece of glass and slashed him across his body. At this point, he was begging for his life. I put the gun to his temple and told him, "If ever there was a good time to pray it was now." I stuck the gun to his head and fired; it was empty, and the click of the gun spelled a reprieve, as relief and disbelief crossed his face. He was shaking with fear and had peed himself. I walked off into the kitchen, thinking, *At least he's now gone through some of the fear Debs felt*. We stole a few things, gagged him, and left him tied as we made our escape.

We got back to Alex's and Julie's place, made some breakfast, then had a hit and forgot about that evening's terrible events. Lunch approached; it was now thirteen hours since we'd left the guy tied up. Much debate followed as we searched our brains about the best way to get him released. I'd just had another crank and laid back in my chair when I heard the doors go in, bang. "Police, stay where you are." I could just about open my eyelids, so staying where I was wasn't a problem to me. There were coppers running backwards and forwards all over the house. I had some downers in my hand and just knew we'd be in custody for a long time. I necked them quick and swallowed and tried to stand. In what seemed like one movement, I was lifted to my feet, to be thrown on the floor, then cuffed behind my back. It was a couple of days before I was fit to be questioned. I went through my mandatory "no comment" routine, then was taken back to my cell. Later that night, we were all charged with robbery and told other charges may follow. The following day, we appeared in the magistrates' court in our white paper boiler suits; there was little point in applying for bail once the prosecution had outlined the more aggravating points of our charge. The magistrate remanded us in custody, and I stepped out of the meat wagon into the reception of the prison, waiting and with time to reflect on events.

Two months had passed, and we were now due to be committed to the crown court for trial. My mum and dad brought some clean clothes to court for me. My poor parents were quite horrified by the circumstances around the case and had pleaded with me to change. I wanted to please them, even end their misery by getting clean, but there was always something else which took priority. Right now, it was my court case. Once we stood before the court, I thought there was no way we'd be given bail. Firstly, because the events of the case were too aggravating, and secondly, we looked a right bunch of undesirables. When the magistrate granted us bail, I could hardly believe my ears. I had to reside at my parents' house and was given a curfew from seven at night 'til seven in the morning. It was good to be home; at least now I was out, I could see my solicitor to get things sorted for the crown. Next day, I met with Alex to go through our depositions. However, once we were off our faces, that went right out the window.

Christmas was fast approaching, and as hard as I tried, I couldn't see myself sticking to my bail conditions over the holiday period. I'd started going out with Sharon, and I was spending a fair bit of time at her place. She was a smart looking bird, a good laugh, but really one of the boys. We got our hands on a wide variety of drugs to see us over the Christmas break so we wouldn't run short. On day two of our seasonal drug bender, I nipped home to get a new works. En route back to Sharon's place, I could see the police car checking me out from a distance as I walked down the road. I didn't want to spend the rest of Christmas banged up so thought losing them would be the best option.

The police car was crawling towards me, doing a few miles an hour, about thirty yards behind when I leapt over the wall to my right, through some gardens and across some allotments. I peered in both directions as I walked through the industrial buildings and crossed the road to the housing estate; everywhere was quiet. Feeling quite pleased with myself that I'd shaken off the police, I turned the corner onto Sharon's street. My heart sank as I heard a police radio crackle; they had me cornered like a rat. There was nowhere for me to run this time; I looked at the arresting officer who'd felt my collar before, "This is becoming too much of a habit; haven't you got better things to do than harass me?" I said.

"No," he replied in a stern voice. The steel of my cubical in the meat wagon felt colder than usual, and as I contemplated my future prospects, so did my heart.

I sat in the cells, beneath the Victorian courthouse, feeling depressed, as I hadn't heard anything from my co-accused, Alex, Julie, and Debs. As far as I was concerned, I was pleading 'not guilty', but didn't know if they'd had a change of heart. Keys were jingling down the corridor, and I heard footsteps, could this be my barrister?

The door opened slowly, and in walked Mr Owen, my brief. "Phil, before we go up for plea, I have something I need to tell you," he said, in his refined way. "Regrettably, there will only be three of you in the dock today. Debbie was found dead in her flat yesterday," he said. Debs had told me she'd thought about ending her life, even so, I was shocked. I questioned myself, "This can't really be happening, Phil, can it?" I walked up the steps into the dock, numb, seeing only Alex and Julie, and guessed it must be that "Not Guilty" were the only words required of me and the only words I could say. Debs was a young woman in her early twenties. Her grief was too much before she was raped, now it was all over for her, no more pain.

Back in Risley, time went fast enough. I got a job cleaning and working on the hot plate, serving food. I received a Dear John from Sharon, which I'd expected, so now I could focus my attention on court. Another four months had passed, and it was the day before the trial. I'd seen my barrister a few weeks previously to iron everything out. It was dinner time, and visiting was usually finished by now. I was serving out this cow pie stuff when my name was shouted, "Grimes, visit, your brief's here!" *How weird*, I thought, *I hope there's no more bad news.* By the time I reached the visiting room, my stomach was turning over, and beads of sweat covered my forehead. "Come in and sit down, Phil." *This sounds ominous*, I thought.

"Your victim has died, Phil, the inquest is tomorrow morning. Depending on what verdict is reached will depend on if you are all charged with murder or not. If it is not linked to the robbery, you will be fine." With that, he stood, shook my hand, and walked to the door. "Nothing more we can do today; see you before court." Everything now had a more serious unreality to it. When I got back to my cell, my pad mate saw the look on my face, "Looks like I'd better skin up, then?" he said.

Sleep eventually came upon me, and in my nightmare, I could see a judge stood in my cell. He banged his hammer down on the table. I could hear him repeating the words, "You will go to prison for life, you will go to prison for life, you will go to prison for life." I woke up for court feeling fully wired, every nerve ending in my body screaming for drugs.

Alex, now in custody, was already sat in the cell reading a newspaper when I arrived from prison. "Eh, Phil, bad news about Debbie," he said. "Still trying to take in," I replied. At twelve o'clock, my barrister appeared at the cell door, "Good news, Phil, the inquest has been heard. You are still charged with robbery at the minute, and now we've been asked if you'd plead guilty to a lesser charge of theft and ABH," he said. This was now sounding good, "Of course, I'll plead to a lesser charge; tell them yes, quick, before they change their minds." I leaned back on the wooden bench and relief washed through my body, at least now I had a future. My mind ran riot, wondering what sentence we'd get. Alex had just come back from a conference with his barrister; he'd been given the same news. I knew by the huge smile that had taken over ninety per cent of his face. We hugged and laughed at how events had spun right round on its head. My barrister started his speech to outline our mitigating circumstances surrounding this whole offence, and to be honest, he didn't have to lay it on. Court was adjourned, and we descended into the cells.

After what felt like an eternity, we were unlocked, and a screw informed us the judge wanted us for sentencing. The only words I remember were, "You shall go to prison for four years." Alex got four years and Julie, his partner, was given two years; we all did quite well, considering. I was allowed a visit after sentencing. This screw who sat in the dock with us and listened to the case sorted it out. "You did well there, Grimesy, lad," he said, as he unlocked the visiting area.

When I saw my parents, they both looked shattered. Mum had been crying, my dad stood beside her looking thoughtful and quiet. "I'll use this time wisely," I said. I really thought I was in control of my life. If I had proved anything in my twenty-one years, it was that I was out of control. I meant what I said at that moment, but I'd made one too many empty promises as far as getting clean was concerned. My dad smiled then winked, "Keep your chin up, Phil; we'll be over to visit when we can." I could hear the screw shouting to wind the visit up, so I looked over to Mum and said, "I'll be home before you know it." Really because I didn't know what to say. I was processed through reception in no time and banged up for the night with two other guys, one who'd got fifteen years for armed robbery and the other a lifer who'd been sent from another prison for an operation. When the guy with fifteen years asked what I'd got in court, "I only got four years, mate," I said, almost apologetically but pleased I didn't have fifteen years stretching out in front of me.

A week later, Alex and I were called back in front of the judge, and he reduced our sentence by a year. Later, I was told by my barrister that people had contacted the courts because we were dealt with harshly; personally, I don't know what the judge's reasons were; I didn't care either.

My time in Walton I spent chasing around for drugs to escape the real prison, the one that existed in my mind where the perimeter wall looked to be unclimbable. I sat in my cell day after day, week after week, month after month, wasted on smack. I saw no alternative. There was absolutely nothing to do but to duck and dive for drugs and tune out; besides, the prison was flooded with them. I had started suffering from nightmares, which made me feel trapped. I found myself locked into a maze where both the roof and the floor were made from glass. The walls that stretched from one to the other were prison walls.

Pink Floyd boomed through the passageways, "All in all you're just another brick in the wall." I ran desperately around the maze to escape the demon that had been set loose. This was the demon of self-destruction; I could feel his breath on my neck, and his eyes bore into the back of my head as he chased me nightly around my dream, never quite fully catching me. God was watching through the glass ceiling and would give me extra strength to keep running, 'cause if the demon of self-destruction caught me and possessed my body, I'd die. Night after night, I would wake from this dream soaked in sweat, gasping for breath, shaking uncontrollably, just before the demon had a chance to bite into the back of my neck. I was left feeling like some psychological gladiator, running for my life. So I roamed the jail, buying up whatever sleeping tablets I could get my hands on, to escape the demon of self-destruction, only to self-destruct.

Heroin didn't switch off the nightmares, only downers. I got involved in stealing some sleepers from the surgery, where meds were given out. The minute this bottle of Ativan arrived on the wing, it was shared out around some of the lads. There wasn't time to knock them out, so we necked them there and then before evening meal was served. When our landing was unlocked, it was obvious to the staff where their drugs had gone.

Some of us were taken down the block and the rest to the strip cells. After a week in a strip cell, I was shipped out to Preston, which in those days was a training nick, where you finished your sentence. I managed to get my hands on drugs, and I used heroin almost every day in Preston, which meant that when I got put on report and sent down the block for two weeks, I rattled for the first week. Once back on the wing, the first thing I'd do was to find out who'd been on a visit.

I was given home leave and was determined to get as smashed as was possible. Kenny had been released already, and when I walked into his flat, he already had my gear waiting on the table, with a spoon and a works ready to go.

I met Tracey who lived a few doors away. She was always laughing, despite her bleak prospects of living in a council-owned maisonette with her three kids, a massive heroin habit, and very little money. I gave her some gear because I felt sorry for her but knew she was a very shrewd cookie. "Call around for a brew later if you want!" she said, as I stood to leave Kenny's place.

I walked back to the jail late after I'd been to collect my parcels of gear. My backside felt like it would burst in two with all the drugs I'd put up there. I walked in the gatehouse and was put on report immediately, so I was back down the block.

My sentence was finished; I had one day left to do. My last night, I lay awake wondering how the future might be different if I took another route. I hoped and prayed there was another road for me to take. But things had to be on my terms, and because they were, I still had some running to do so I could keep a healthy distance in front of the demon of self-destruction.

Chapter Fourteen

I was twenty-four now, and time was on my side. I walked from the prison gate to the street, only to disappear like a ghost into the mist that was the drug scene to score some more.

I called around at Tracey's flat for that cup of tea and ended up staying for dinner. Tracey had three young kids, Kathy, Andrew, and Paul. Once they'd shown me all their toys and played hide and seek, I then read them a bedtime story, and they went up to bed very reluctantly. We shared some gear, talked, listened to some Pink Floyd, and I stayed over.

Tracey and I had a mutual friend who I knew well from prison; he was calling around the following day to take her to score in Manchester. I still had my discharge grant in my pocket so asked if I could come along for the ride.

Johnny was from Moss Side originally, so we had a better chance of not getting ripped off. In Manchester, we pulled down a street of terraced houses and waited. We were sat there for only ten minutes when a Rasta opened the rear door and jumped in the car. We scored an ounce of heroin and headed back to Blackpool. In Tracey's flat, I stuck a green spike into my groin and drew back the plunger, watching as a cloud of thick red blood mushroomed into the barrel. I pushed the gear in to find my good friend heroin bringing me the sense of well-being that only he had to offer. Later in the evening, I put another hit together; Tracey and the kids were at her mum's. When I pushed the gear in, I got an intense pain rip through me; I dropped to the floor ridged and with an arched back. It was as if my kidneys were being squeezed. My temples pounded, bang, bang.

I thought my head would explode at any minute. I had pins and needles in my legs which were going numb, and my skin was on fire. I'd never had a dirty hit before but had heard plenty about them from other addicts. I thought, *If I'm dying, I don't want to be conscious of it,* and I was able to get into my back pocket for some downers. I managed to swallow them, and after what seemed like half an hour, I could feel them working. I woke up where I'd fallen the previous night, covered in vomit which had set hard in my hair. I didn't know if my dirty hit was due to what the heroin was cut with or if it was a fibre from the filter I'd used. It could have been either.

Tracey was sat in the chair across from me smoking a cigarette with a concerned look on her face. "What happened to you Phil, did you go over?" Once I explained, she told me she'd tried to get me up off the floor but couldn't lift me.

We bagged up the gear ready to sell and afterwards put what we'd made to one side. I thought I'd leave off injecting for a while, give my body a rest and smoke it from the foil. The next few weeks were a haze of heroin, alcohol, weed, and sex when I could manage it. Tracey had been to see her doctor who gave her Palfium and Seconal, then stopped off at her friend's for a drink. She walked in the flat with a blank expression on her face. She put her handbag on the table. "Did you get them or what?" I asked. "Yes, I got them, and by the way, you're going to be a dad!"

She was a few weeks pregnant with my baby; I was totally blown away. We'd only been together a couple of months. I sat thinking about what Tracey had told me and some of the implications of it all. No way was I ready to be a father. I really needed to do something to get my head together. I would have to get myself registered at the CDT and see what they could do for me. Tracey and I sat outside the doctor's room in the drug team building, noting the depressed look on the faces of those who'd already been in to see the doctor. Our turn came, and we sat down across from this Asian guy. I told him I was recently released from prison and had already got myself a habit, and now my girlfriend was pregnant. He looked at me in disbelief, then went on to tell me how irresponsible I'd been and that there was a high possibility of social services involvement from the start. I already knew I'd been irresponsible and had gone to ask if they could advise me on where to look for help. I hadn't anticipated a sermon. "Look, Doctor, we don't want to carry on using heroin, it's shite." He made a couple of phone calls, and now we were on the list for detox, and he gave us both a Methadone script. I had started to see our situation more clearly as time went by, and I'd got into the habit of taking the Methadone daily.

We walked into the detox unit and looked around at the place. I had watched a film on television about a Victorian lunatic asylum only the week before, and it was a very grim tale. Now I was in the real thing, for eight to twelve weeks. Our stuff was searched, then we were given our meds. The nurse filled a large test tube with Methadone, then another test tube with Diazepam, which was in a thick pink solution and took ages to leave the bottle. As it landed in the test tube, I gipped at the thought of swallowing the stuff.

I talked with the nurse, as I was confused about the amount I was given because I knew I'd have to do my rattle sooner or later. She reassured me that I had been given the right dose.

A week had passed, and Tracey and I were informed by the head nurse we could now go out around the village if we wanted, for an hour. Four of us set off for a walk in the grounds; it would take us half an hour to cross the hospital. The hospital had its own little village with a café and shops, and we'd decided to go and try out the hospital's own coffee. We sat down around our table and sipped on our drinks. The conversation soon turned to drugs, who'd used what, where, and when. Vic, the guy sat opposite, said he'd had enough of rattling and wanted to use. He was from Manchester and made a phone call and arranged to meet his dealer in the grounds the following day. Tracey and I were stable on the more than generous amount of drugs we were being given and hadn't started to be reduced off it yet. We were finishing our drinks when this enormous woman ran across to our table, looking quite distressed, pointing to a crumpled up old photograph in her hand. She weighed what appeared to be getting on for twenty stone, so when she launched herself onto my knee, my legs almost gave way. She pointed at the photograph, telling me it was hers, and no one would ever take this away. At that point, she stuck her lips onto mine and started to kiss me. I desperately tried to pull my head away but to no avail as a claustrophobic sensation gripped me; the smell of body odour and damp clothing made me retch, and I could only hear the laughter of those around my table. A male nurse appeared and started to pull her off me. This made me even more freaked out, and she was now screeching loudly. Every head in the place was now turned in my direction. She jumped to her feet, it seemed when she was ready and ran out the door.

When we returned, I flew straight to the bathroom to frantically brush my teeth and was gobsmacked when a nurse came in and asked me if I'd had any alcohol. I could hear the laughter from the other side of the door and tried to explain my encounter in the café but couldn't for laughing. Tracey shouted to the nurse outside the bathroom and told her of my plight. I walked into the office to hand in a urine sample; there was a staff handover taking place, which consisted of them rolling around laughing at me and my new, so-called girlfriend, who they all knew very well. Apparently, she'd been in the hospital forty years after having an illegitimate child.

After two weeks, Tracey was feeling restless, and my view of detox had gone down the pan. Vic had been discharged for using on the premises, and we agreed to give him a call and arrange for him to drop off some gear. That night, we waited in my room watching through the window for Vic. He showed up twenty minutes after the arranged time, puffing and panting; he'd run from the main gate. He gave us our two bags, a works, and some citric and said he'd meet us at the café the next day. We thought we may still have a bit of heroin showing in our urine samples and could argue the toss if there wasn't. I was feeling particularly rough the last few days, as our Meth was reduced. We had our gear and felt brand new again, physically, but the guilt of our baby feeling what we felt weighed heavily on me.

Staying away from the staff proved to be more of a challenge than we'd realised. I was convinced we'd been rumbled, but Tracey said it was just me being paranoid. I went into town with a member of staff the following morning to cash my benefit book. When I returned, I was told Tracey had been discharged. She was asked to give a random urine sample and was sussed out.

I stood in the toilet, peeing into a pot, knowing that I'd be asked to leave shortly. I lay on my bed glancing out the window, waiting to be asked to leave, but no one came. The Chinese guy who walked around the building all day was doing his usual circles. He wore a black Stetson hat and a long black overcoat; he looked a mysterious character, and I wondered what had landed him in here. His eyes were unblinking and glazed by medication, screaming out loneliness and were fixed ahead. I sat and reflected on some of the events that had taken place since I left jail.

Everything appeared to happen so quickly, and in a few months' time, I'd be a dad. I felt totally out of control over my situation; I was powerless, powerless over my drug taking; however, I was not ready for throwing in the towel just yet. I wanted to fight. I thought, *I'll surrender myself to rehab when I am good and ready to stop, not when a probation officer, judge, or drug worker tells me to.* I'd been told by others who'd done that, that it doesn't work if it's to please a parent or the wife. It has to be for yourself because if you hit a tough time and they aren't around for you, eventually, you'd use. I used two days later and was asked to leave the unit. I returned to our flat where Tracey was cooking up a hit. I felt guilty when I used; it made me feel responsible for Tracey using, and when Tracey used heroin, our baby would have felt this.

I would have never considered giving drugs to a child, and this was no different. This feeling of guilt wouldn't go away; only more drugs would take this away. Even then, that would be temporary, at best. I walked into the maternity suite where Tracey was lying on the bed, asking me for drugs. I couldn't believe my ears; I had four peach Palfium in my pocket. I threw them across the room and launched into an argument, screaming names at each other, at which point, a nurse came in and asked me to leave and wait outside.

Sarah was born addicted to Methadone and was taken from her mother into the special care baby unit. I looked into my daughter's incubator and saw this beautiful baby girl twitching and making high-pitched screaming noises, as she withdrew from the drug. I hated myself and felt a deep sense of shame, while this helpless, vulnerable little baby entered this world to contend with something so horrible that she didn't ask for. I stood over her day after day crying and wishing that things could have been different for her. Sarah was a little fighter, and after weeks in the hospital, she was now home.

We now had a new house, on a different estate, which was a good move. We'd been there a few weeks, and the health visitor told us that she would call back the following day and we would meet our new social worker. Claire, the social worker, called the next day and stated her position with us.

She was relatively new at the job and hadn't long finished at university. This didn't exactly fill me with confidence in her, and it left me thinking, *What does she know about our situation, parenting, and drug abuse? All this woman has done is pass exams and read books.* I realised that social workers wielded a fair amount of power and hoped that she wouldn't be wielding it in our directions.

It was summer, and the weather was great, so I decided to have a go at fixing the front door. I had a hammer and chisel in hand, chipping away a bump on the doorframe so that hopefully it would close easier. I became aware of someone behind me at the gate. I turned to see this guy standing there who I didn't really like. I had read the newspaper write up which told of how he'd gone Queen's evidence on someone else whom I didn't know, but nevertheless, wasn't happy about. I had prided myself on what now seems to be an old-fashioned value that you didn't grass under any circumstances. As he didn't hold the same values as me, I didn't trust him. "What do you want around here?" I asked in a lowered tone. "Do you know where there's any drugs, Phil?" he shouted. I stood there gripping my hammer, quietly fuming, when he shouted the same remark again.

"Phil, do you know who's got any gear?" I looked up to see my new neighbours, next but one, who were in the garden shaking their heads and tutting. I ran down the garden, gripping my hammer tightly, chasing him down the street, swinging my hammer at the back of his head, and as I reached the junction, I stopped and watched as he sped past the shocked onlookers who were stood at the bus stop.

Tracey had already heard about our visitor from someone on the street and was pleased he wouldn't be calling back. We turned in for bed that night, making sure Sarah was safely tucked up in her Moses basket, and we went to sleep.

I felt a real dull pain in my head before I attempted to open my eyes, and as my vision cleared, there was a man dressed in black wearing a balaclava stood pointing a gun at my head and another guy wearing the same at the other end of the bed. The pain in my head had become intense, and I guessed the warm sensation on my face was blood which was now pooling on my chest.

The guy next to the bed was screaming, "You're fucking dead; you're fucking dead!" It was at this point I realised that when I was getting pistol-whipped that the gun would have been levelled at Sarah's cot. Both Tracey and I had sussed out who one of them was, and he wasn't known for his bravery. It was the guy I had words with the day before. We spent the next five minutes telling them they would get serious bird for this, so they'd be better off doing a building society and at least have something to show for it. This worked, and they fled the house. I was whisked off to hospital five minutes later when the police swamped the house and radioed an ambulance. The police tried questioning me in hospital, but I was saying nothing. I wanted my own revenge, plus I wanted to get home and make sure my daughter and stash were safe. A few days after, I was told the guy concerned was now in Spain working, so that was the end of that, for now.

As time went on, Tracey became ill and couldn't look after the children, so they were taken into temporary foster care. I was slightly relieved, as I'd been looking after her three kids and Sarah and was also frightened they wouldn't let us have them back. They did come back eight weeks later, and nothing much had changed. We were still taking the same old same old, and if it were possible, sinking further into even more of a state. It was getting increasingly harder to hit my groin since I now had a large ball of gristle in front of the vein, which had formed as a consequence of the continual prodding of the vein. So, I had to stab through that to get a hit. Painful yes, but I had to do it. This one day, I had put three peach Palfium into my groin and was sat on the settee talking to myself in my usual slurred way while the kids were playing in the other room, and Sarah was in her pram by the window. Tracey was out scoring, so I had some time before I had to get my head together. When I came around, I put another hit together. I leaned backwards against the living room wall, dropped my trousers to the floor, and I was still quite stoned, so I never checked the colour of the blood in my works. I knew it was in the vein, so I put it in. I noticed the burning sensation within seconds, as I felt my foot grow in size and that shooting pain that I remembered from years ago when I nearly lost my hand. By the next day, both my legs were so swollen they looked like Cumberland sausages, and the realisation that I needed to get to the hospital was a depressing thought.

I told the doctor in the accident and emergency department what I had done. He recoiled with disgust when I told him that when I pulled the syringe from my groin, blood had spurted from one side of the room to the other. Fear had now started to grip me when his face changed from one that was friendly to one of anger and judgement. I wondered if I should have told the truth or not. I was put on a drip straight away and taken by wheelchair up to a ward. The doctor had told me what I already knew; I'd injected into an artery. The pain in my legs exhausted me, and my temperature was now dangerously high. I was given a variety of painkilling tablets and Methadone, which didn't kill the pain but did fry my brain. I could only lie down and hope the pain would go, and eventually, I would fall asleep. I was due to see my consultant this day, which was a strained relationship to say the least. His opinion of me was like all junkies: we should be put on an island and blown up because we were a tremendous drain on the NHS. He was a small, slim guy who dressed immaculately and spoke the Queen's English;

however, the inside of the man did not mirror the outer appearance.

Three weeks had dragged by, and I had become progressively worse. My legs were more swollen, and the pain had increased. The consultant, Mr Wild, arrived with his team and a couple of junior doctors. He approached my bed, giving me a look as though he could have easily scraped me from the sole of his shoe. "Mr Grimes, I really am at a loss as the best way forward in dissolving these clots. I have thought long and hard about this and think we should look at amputation." For once, I was speechless. He took a silver pen from his jacket pocket and started to draw on my thigh, telling me how he would cut the leg away in a V-shape, leaving two ends left to sew together to create a stump... "And by the way, I just need a signature from you giving your consent for the operation."

"Not a fucking chance; no way am I letting you chop my leg off!" I said. "There has got to be something else you could do instead, no way, no way." And with that, he shook his head, tutting loudly. "As you wish, Mr Grimes. I will explore other options." He spun around on his heal and slipped through the curtain. The nurse who'd been designated to look after me was busy attending to someone else and heard what had been said, came in, and asked me if I wanted medication. She brought my painkillers and stood in front of me to make sure I'd swallowed them. I opened my mouth to show her they had gone; she smiled and walked away.

When I was sure she was in the office and out of site, I spat them into the top pocket of my pyjamas. I had done the same thing at breakfast; so now I had four Diconal for a hit. I swung my body to the edge of the bed and lowered my myself into the wheelchair, careful so as not to bang my leg. I hopped from my chair into a cubical and injected into the very same leg the consultant had drawn on. Veins that were once deep in my thighs had now come up to the surface, due to the blockage of the clot. My trips to the toilet had become longer and longer, so it was no real surprise when one day after I'd used, I could hear the ward sister hammering on the toilet door. I quickly tried to pull myself together, but this lady was no fool, and although she could prove nothing, she had an idea what was going on.

Two days had passed since the encounter in the toilet with the nurse, and as I looked down the ward, I could see the doctor from the CDT now talking to the sister. What could he be doing here? I wondered. He was a bald Asian guy with an incredibly big nose, so there was no mistaking him. His work suit was shiny with creases that made it look like he might have slept wearing it. He glanced my way to see me staring at him in disbelief. I made my way down the ward in my chair, squeaking loudly. Someone had let my tyres down on my wheelchair, I was certain it was the ward sister trying to put a stop to my visits to the toilet. He was all smiles when he sat down across the table from me. "Now Phillip, I am a little concerned with the medication you are on. You appear to be on massive amounts of painkillers, and we need to adjust this to something more manageable." His do-gooder tactics had got my hackles up from the word go, and I could feel a rage descending on me towards this man. "Doctor, that's because, believe it or not, I'm in great pain," I said.

"Phillip, Diconal, DF118, Methadone, and Nembutal is a dangerous combination in these amounts. For a start, I'm going to have your Diconal made into syrup for you and finish you on the Dihydrocodeine." It was now plain to me he'd been invited along by the hospital to spoil my fun if you could call it that. I leapt from my chair, onto my good leg, over to where he was sitting with my medical records on his lap. I grabbed my records, which he was now grasping with all his might, and we started to wrestle. He wasn't for letting go, and my hopping on one leg didn't do anything for my technique.

Papers were flying everywhere, and he was shouting "Phillip, Phillip behave yourself!" I knew I couldn't keep this up for much longer, as I had no energy or balance. Behind Dr Khan was a walk-in type of stockroom, so I pushed him towards it with my last bit of strength, not really meaning to knock him over or hurt him. Books and files were falling from the shelf above him, covering him in paper as he sat on his backside. I shut the door quickly and locked it and tossed the key through the open window. I could hear his muffled shouts behind me, "Phillip, come on; open the door!" I couldn't help chuckling to myself. I climbed back in my chair, made for the second door and pulled it to behind me. Dr Khan was discovered two hours later when his office called the hospital, concerned as to his whereabouts. Two nurses came and asked me what time he left. "Could he still be in there?" I asked, with a smirk on my face.

"Why don't you have a look, nurse?" I said, unable to hide my amusement. I followed them down the ward to the room where I'd left him. They opened the door, and I heard a faint voice.

"Please. Please, I'm needing the toilet."

It took the hospital maintenance staff half an hour to show up, then a further twenty minutes to get him out. The wet patch on his trouser leg told that he didn't need the toilet now. He was not a happy man once freed from his cupboard, so I thought I'd best make myself scarce.

The following day, I was moved to Withington hospital in Manchester. My consultant was an expert in the area of veins and arteries. He adjusted my anticoagulants and put me under a physiotherapist. Within ten days, I was on my feet. A few days later, I was making trips to the day room. A week later, I was allowed to go home. I'm so pleased I didn't sign Mr Wild's consent form for amputation.

Back home, the kids were out of foster care, and Tracey was feeling better now she'd had a break from us all, so we could get back to some sense of normality, whatever that was. This was short-lived, as a couple of weeks later, Tracey went downhill again, not helped by her continual consumption of drugs of every description. The kids were back in foster care, which saddened me. I desperately wanted to get my act together now, for the kids' sake if nothing else. I went to see my probation officer and told him I was ready for rehab.

Chapter Fifteen

I walked back through the door of the detox unit, determined to see this rattle through. Christmas was not a happy occasion other than the back of it. I had spent the day under my duvet, freezing cold, when one of the nurses walked in and sat down next to my bed. "Your probation officer is supposed to be collecting you on the tenth of January; well, they phoned to say they have a vacancy tomorrow if you want to go. Your key worker will take you; only thing is you'll have to cut your detox short."

I was due to finish my Methadone the following day. The detox unit wanted my bed, and I knew I would have to go sooner or later. I just needed to know I would be able to cope, but I would find out sooner or later.

We pulled in off the main road, into the grounds of a huge house that was Phoenix House, and I was dwarfed by the massive doorway with its handle that was designed for a giant, not me. A tall, thin guy with a shaved head and dark rings like mine took me into the wood panelled office and told me to sit down. Someone else took my bag to be searched, and I looked through the office window at the highly polished bannister rail.

The whole place was very grand with the kings of England carved around a spectacular fireplace, secret panels, a big lawn with a wooded area behind. The fascination with my surroundings came to an abrupt end when the door opened, and this thick-set lad with a Brummie accent shouted over, "You're sharing a room with me, Phil. Come and put your clothes away!" A bell rang, and people were rushing everywhere. After dinner, I was introduced to my peers who I'd go through the programme with. Mick and his girlfriend, Andrea, were from Macclesfield. They were still rattling and told me they were blown away with the regime. Gareth was a social worker from Toxteth, who'd got stuck to the end of a crack pipe. He found great amusement in taking on staff about their approach to treatment. He'd often explained to me the reasons behind what seemed like a bizarre programme with bizarre consequences.

New Year's Eve, two minutes before midnight, and all forty of us were stood outside this mock Tudor mansion, with a candle each to hold. The wind whistled through the trees that surrounded us, and I could see their dark silhouettes against the starlit sky. They swayed from side to side under the forces of nature. We each lit our candles and held them up. The director of the rehab had come along and gave a moving speech about adversity, change, and the hope of a drug-free future. It was rounded off by music from Peter Gabriel and Kate Bush singing, "Don't Give Up." We all hugged, then went to bed.

The following morning, we were awoken early and told to get our breakfasts, then assemble outside the group room. There was to be a marathon. I was feeling extremely rough at this point and wondered how I'd ever make it to breakfast, let alone go running. I wrapped myself in a quilt and went to voice my concerns to the expeditor; this was another resident who helped organise people. I was shivering now with a running nose and a head full of insanity. The expeditor was stressed and often abused the power his position brought him. "There is no fucking way I'm running anywhere today, Ged, I'm too ill," I protested.

"Phil, you are not going to be running anywhere looking at you, except maybe the toilet. And anyway, this is a marathon group meeting, not cross country," he said, laughing and shaking his head. I was glad he saw the humour of my situation and understood that those new through the door may not have the zeal for therapy some of the older hands displayed. I stood shaking and twitching outside the group room. Ged, the expeditor, approached me and put some face paint crayons in my hand. "Phil, I want you to go to your room with Howard and paint your face the way you saw yourself out on the street. Don't think too long about it, or put what you think we want to see; just do it." I sat looking at my reflection in the mirror and took the black crayon from the packet. I plastered the black across the top of my eye like mascara, then put it up to the corner of my mouth and drew a line down under my jaw. Then to finish it off, I put tears from the corner of my eye going on to my cheekbone. I headed back towards the group room, and a blindfold was placed around my eyes, and I was led by the arm into the room where I was asked to kneel. I lowed myself down onto my aching knees.

The wooden floor felt hard against my bones, and now I felt frighteningly vulnerable. I could hear others kneeling around me who were voicing their concern also. Suddenly, music ripped through the room; I recognised the guitar straight away: it was the intro to "Heroin" by Lou Reed. I used this track as part of my ritual when I mixed up my gear. This was holy music in the ears of my god, heroin. Almost immediately, sweat covered my forehead and the palms of my hands. Saliva rushed to my tongue. My thoughts were now swamped with ideas of scoring drugs, and I became aware of a picture of a syringe filling with blood; the dark substance in the barrel was heroin. As the blindfold was removed, I saw two men standing in the middle of the large empty room, one dressed as the Devil, the other as an angel. I watched the first guy stand to his feet; he was made to walk in a circle in the middle of the room, as the Devil taunted him with reminders from his past, from his records. "What about the time you stole money from your girlfriend's bag, and the kids had nothing to eat for days. Then there was the time you stole your mother's painkillers when she was dying from cancer, leaving her racked with pain," he said in an accusing manner. Once the guy was sufficiently wound up like a coiled spring, he was guided over to a large mirror that stood against the wall. Everything that had just happened had distracted him from his recent artwork, and when he saw his face painted, he broke down in tears. The next up was a young woman, and she flipped out in the mirror after the Devil had finished with her.

There were four of us who remained sitting; now it was our turn. I could feel the anxiety in my chest like it would rip it in two pieces. I stood up, now feeling dizzy and walked slowly around in the circle with the Devil on my back. He launched into me, "You have ripped off your mum your dad and just about everyone around you. And I'm not just talking about money. I'm talking emotionally, mentally; you have taken everything from everyone who loves you, and in return, you have given them nothing but worry, fear, dread, stress, and the agony as you selfishly make them watch as you kill yourself." I had heard enough by now and walked to the mirror. I was shocked to see what was looking back and screamed loudly as though a demon was getting exorcised from my soul. Tears now covered my face, and I now felt empty and drained, along with a sore throat from screaming at myself. Once I had gone through this process, I was taken by the angel over to the other side of the room, where the quilts from our beds had been laid. I was told to lie down on a quilt, and the angel brought me a cup of tea, and when we'd all been done, the angel played "Bridge Over Troubled Water" for us. I rolled a cigarette and reflected on my experience with the Devil; we knew each from old, but not like this. His job was to destroy my life, and he was doing a pretty good job by all accounts. If I'd have realised this, I maybe wouldn't have cooperated as much. This good and evil metaphor made a lot of sense from where I sat; only trouble was it seemed almost too simplistic an answer to the path I'd chosen. And what about personal responsibility? Or was I just a pawn in a twisted game of chess, influenced by some spiritual entity from afar? I knew I had made choices, some good, most bad, and after all, if it was a spiritual battle wouldn't you decide which side you were to fight on? Maybe I had unconsciously chosen darkness over light; now I was becoming aware of a struggle happening on a deeper level, and if God was real, and actually listening, why had he never helped me?

This one group left my head cabbaged; I had so many questions that I couldn't get answers to. It was three o'clock in the morning when my light was switched on. It was as if someone was shining a spotlight in my eyes. I could hear a voice in the distance calling my name, but it all seemed like a weird dream. "Phil, Phil, I was dreaming about the angel and Devil, discussing my case with their boss — God and hadn't realised that God spoke in a scouse accent." It was Gareth who was now shaking my arm, "Come on mate, we have to go to the downstairs bogs and wait there." Eventually, I staggered from my bed, threw some clothes on and went to the toilets, not fully convinced this whole thing wasn't a wind-up. The whole community was there, and there was silence, so I was thinking something really serious had gone down.

One at a time we were shown into the toilet with a staff member and the expediter. My turn came, and I was shocked when I was asked if I knew anything about who had done a pee on the toilet seat.

At first, I was angry, but then I saw the funny side of it. They didn't, however, and I was told they would get back to me about my inappropriate outburst of humour. We waited another hour before someone stuck their hand up to it.

The following day, as a consequence for laughing, I had to clean the toilets all day from eight till eight at night.

And on the hour every hour, talk to someone about my feelings. I'd never really shared my feelings with anyone and had found a real release when doing so. I experienced everything from extreme resentment, anger, frustration, fear, and a deep sadness whilst just scrubbing those loos out.

This was a whole new thing to me because I'd turned my feelings on and off with drugs; now there were people who genuinely wanted to know what was going on inside of me. I settled into the routine of the house, and for the first time in ages, started to feel good about myself. The withdrawals had come to an end. I'd even put a few pounds on.

I was getting ready to go to work when the manager came in the room and sat down next to me, "Phil, Tracey has had the children removed from her, and they are in local authority care. I'm very sorry." Her words came like a sledgehammer in the face. I was in here getting myself sorted, and now this. Fear gripped me, and I imagined my daughter growing up not knowing her dad. "I know what I'll do," I said to myself. "I'll leave rehab tomorrow, and at least I can be nearer to them and visit." I spoke with Gareth about it, and he told me that I would be making a bad situation worse and that the best thing I could do was stay here and get myself better, then I'd be in a position to do something positive, so I stayed put.

I went to visit my daughter in Blackpool with a member of staff. We went to the children's home; a huge place in its own grounds. When I talked to the staff about how my daughter had settled in, I was told she cried a lot at first but had now adapted to the routine of the home. Sarah toddled through to the room where we sat. It took a few moments for her to realise who I was, then a beautiful smile lit up her little face; we had a big cuddle, and she was off to fetch me her toys.

On the way back to Phoenix House, I felt bad about leaving Sarah in the home; not that I was in a position to do anything at that moment.

As my head and my heart had started to thaw out from the effects of my drug taking, I started to feel new feelings and see things differently. I knew that my relationship with Tracey was purely based around drugs and nothing else. There was no love, no care, and certainly no honesty. In fact, I didn't know why we were together. When I got the opportunity, I would tell her this. I had even started to believe I could have a future without being in a relationship with a woman or with drugs.

I had been talking with Tracey on the phone and told her we were over. I got to sit and think about our conversation, then I turned to my very own conversation within me, which went a bit like: *Well, Phil, you have been in here for a few months now, and I think you need to leave, 'cause you are strong enough to cope.* Then along came another voice into the debating room, *Yeah Phil, give your head a shake, anyone can hide away in a place like this; it's out there where it counts. You've done what you came to Phoenix to do; now go home.* I sat for a while with my thoughts, not sharing anything with the others in the room, and frustration came upon me as I thought about my circumstances. I made the decision to leave and even believe the lies I'd told myself. I felt saddened to leave the friends I'd made, but there was a buzz going inside me on an unconscious level because I'd decided to use. I sat with my head pressed against the window of the train looking at the shapes I could make with my breath. I knew I was doing the wrong thing, but now I was away from rehab, the urge to use was now so powerful, I knew I had no energy to fight it, so I surrendered.

I sat in my room, in my usual chair, a key around my ankle, a works half-filled with blood sticking from my foot. I looked around and saw on the table an empty spoon, an empty packet of cigarettes, an empty can of Tennent's Super; my reflection in the window showed me an empty man. I felt weird, half of my head was still full of therapy, and I needed more drugs than usual to switch off my feelings. I wished these feelings of guilt and shame would leave me alone. I got another bag and hoped that this would hit the spot. I needed to escape my thoughts of rehab and disappointment in myself, so I took some downers, ah, that's better. I woke up in hospital feeling spaced out. Immediately knowing what had happened, my tolerance level to opiates had dropped whilst I had been in rehab, and I'd gone over. I jumped from my bed and decided to look for my clothes. Suddenly, I felt a sharp pain in my neck and was catapulted back towards the bed. I glanced up and noticed a drip stand with a tube connected to the side of my neck. I felt very dizzy and disorientated, "Got to get out of this place," I say to myself. "I am confused, and my head is foggy, and now my heart is pounding as panic and paranoia take over. Who else knows I'm here? Will this be fed back to the social worker? Will they ever let me get my daughter out of care?" I left the hospital and made my way around to see Tracey. She would be able to give me an update on what was happening with the kids. The door opened, and I saw an old friend standing there. I heard my daughter crying in the background. "I can't let you in Phil, and the kids don't want to see you." I couldn't suss it out straight away, then I worked it out. Tracey and Kev must be seeing each other. "I want to see my daughter, Kev, and you can't stop me," I said, angry now at the situation. Tracey came to the door telling me that she couldn't have the kids as long as she was living with me. I started to walk away, feeling totally gutted about what I'd just been told. Tracey had a raging habit, and Kev was out of control at the best of times; how come I was so bad? I'd speak to the social worker myself and get access.

After a long discussion with the social worker, she agreed for me to have supervised visits with Sarah at my parents, once a week until I got somewhere to live and got my drug use under control, whatever that was supposed to mean.

Now I only had myself to think about, not that I really thought about anyone else anyway. I decided to get away for a while. I'd been talking with a mate who had recently arrived back from Amsterdam. He brought back some E's and coke which he had done nicely from. *That's what I'll do; get over to Holland and do my rattle there.* Not one of my best plans, I have to admit.

Chapter Sixteen

It was snowing heavily when the coach neared Folkestone. I jabbed the spike through my jeans, wincing as I pressed the plunger down. I knew my meth amps wouldn't last forever, but I could score once we'd arrived in Amsterdam. I had a few hundred pounds in my jacket pocket that would see me through the first few days.

On the coach down to Folkestone, I chatted with two young women who were also looking to sleep rough. So we agreed to stick together for safety.

Angie and Pippa were at Liverpool University and had taken time out from their studies to see some of Europe. We walked around for a couple of hours looking for somewhere covered to doss down. We came across a drop-in centre attached to a church, so called in for a rest. The clientele was a mixture of students, travellers, and other drug users.

A guy on the next table asked me how long it would be before we'd be fed. "Not got a clue," I replied. "Do you know any decent places where we can crash?" I asked. "Yeah man, there's a network of tunnels under Central Station, past the lockers area. If you can get down there without staff clocking you, it's really warm and safe," he said in a strong Irish accent. "By the way, are you three looking to score?" His words were music to my ears. "Yeah, I am, let's go and talk outside," I said.

"No, not so fast. I'm not going outside; I'll serve you here!"

I locked myself in the cubicle with my half gram of china white. I loaded my works with less gear than usual, knowing this stuff was strong. The rush started with a beautiful warmth then a calm that only angels bring. I'd wedged myself into the corner so I didn't collapse forward, and my last thoughts were, *This would be a beautiful way to die.* My magic carpet delivered me from the ugly reality which had become my life as I wandered off into a corner of heaven and dreamed of another place. I didn't know how long I'd been there or even where I was. *Bang, bang, bang!* I opened my eyes to see the toilet door shake. "Are you OK in there?" shouted a concerned voice in broken English. "Yeah be with you in a few minutes, just nodded off, I've not slept for three days," I said. I managed to pull myself together and walked unsteadily into the drop-in area, to see Angie and Pippa getting up to leave. "Where've you been? We've waited over two hours. Come on, get it together, we've got to go and check out these tunnels at the train station."

Once we had sneaked past rows and rows of lockers, we came to a dimly-lit tunnel. Making left and right turns until we'd walked for about ten minutes, we found what we thought would be a good spot, and I laid my backpack down, undid my sleeping bag, and stretched out. It was lovely and warm, with the occasional rumble of a train and high-pitched squeals because of the pipes that ran along the back wall. The rats were the only reminder of the world that I was in a hurry to blot out. I sat hunched over with my belt around my ankle, my foot on the warm pipe, searching for a vein in the sole of my foot, "Got ya." Pippa was sitting, writing postcards to her friends, whilst skinning up and talking with Angie. I soon fell into a deep sleep.

A sharp burning pain exploded in my ribs which caused me to gasp for breath. I looked up at the dark figures which stood to my side and could see the semi-automatic weapon he was pointing at me, "On your feet and move on." He didn't have to say anything else; his gun said it all. Now separated from Angie and Pippa, the rest of the night was spent wandering around the Red-Light District until I found some steps to rest on. I was drifting in and out of sleep when I heard a gentle and kind voice speaking to me, "You won't be able to stay there much longer; the police will move you on. Or if my boss sees you there, it will be worse for you. Try the De vas, you will get a bed there and something to eat." She was tall, with long brown hair and seemed older than her years. "Let me know how you go on! I work over there in that window." And with that, she hurried off into the misty morning. Later that day, I joined the queue outside De vas. The huge grey building fitted in nicely with my mood. There was still snow on the ground, and my feet were frozen. My ankles and legs were ulcerated.

Gaping holes, which now burned and sent electric shocks upwards, made me even more determined to score some gear. It didn't take long to score in the queue. We'd stood outside most of the afternoon, then a guy with keys appeared. The rush to get in was the worst brawl I'd seen in a long time. Feet and fists, snot and blood, flew everywhere. One poor sod screamed as he was crushed underfoot. As I made it through the doors, I breathed a sigh of relief. I turned to see if I could spot the two lads I'd scored off. No, they must be in the building; there were only two people left now the doors were shut. One guy who was talking to himself, another kid who was stood there crying at the prospect of another night on the cruel streets of Amsterdam.

We queued again for another hour, as we waited for our number to be called.

I walked into a large white tiled room with a big long table in the middle, around the outside were shower cubicles. I was told to sit down, and a worker took some details from me. Then further down the table, I surrendered all my belongings and my clothes which stunk by now. I walked further down, and another worker gave me my new attire which was a white hospital theatre gown and a pair of flip-flops and was told to queue at the shower. The first cubicle was a red-hot shower; the ulcers on my legs and ankles screamed at me as the water soaked through my makeshift bandage. The next thing I was pelted with delousing powder which burned my eyes. Covered from head to toe in white dust, wearing my theatre gown and flip-flops, I shuffled along past a guy who was having his head shaved, to receive a bowl of soup and a bun. The soup smelled heavenly but looked like a swamp. I didn't care; I was just so grateful for some food by now. I walked through into the dining area and looked around for a seat when I noticed one to my right. The guy sat at the table looked seriously angry like he was committing murders in his head. He was a huge guy, maybe 19 stone, who looked like he worked out. His jet black, cropped hair and furrowed brow added to his menacing appearance. I stuck my hand towards him, "My name's Phil."

"OK, Phil, I'm Harry," came his reply in a strong American accent. By now his smile filled his face, and he threw a pack of Marlboro onto the table top, "Help yourself." Harry went on to tell me his story. His family had moved from Holland when he was a baby. So he'd grown up and gone to school there, and it was there that he had got involved with organised crime on a large scale. He had just finished a fifteen-year stretch in the penitentiary and had now been deported, not to return back to America for 20 years. His wife and three children would follow him in a few weeks' time. As he spoke, a tear fell down his cheek. The one thing we now had in common was we were both on our arses in De vas, and wearing our ridiculous theatre gowns, with our backsides hanging out, and silly flip flops. I had to laugh at the situation, and the bizarre circumstances, humour and bravado had never failed me, at least so far.

That night, I slept in-between crisp, clean sheets on a bed fit for a king; it was sheer bliss.

In the early hours of the morning, I felt someone shaking me. "Fuck off!" I screamed, but they persisted. Now I'm the kind of person who loves his sleep, and this guy by now was screaming it was his bed, and I should move. I threw my hands up, "OK, OK, have your bed." I jumped up as if to leave, and as he drew level, I headbutted him on the temple. He dropped to the floor, and that was that. I dragged him to the toilets then got back to bed and thought no more of it.

When I left in the morning, I was told not to come back. *Place was a doss hole anyway*, I thought. Blaming others came naturally.

Next day, I met up with Harry, the yank. Harry put me in touch with a friend where I might get some work. My first job was a sneak on what looked like a law firm. That went well. I don't know what was in the case, but I got a grand for lifting it. Money meant Heroin, and that was all I cared about. I was in a strange country and one that could be hostile. I wondered what my mum and dad were doing; I loved them dearly and hated myself for hurting them. I was one selfish bastard. So I got wasted. That night, I met my new boss in a bar. I sat with him having a drink and smoking weed, listening to reggae. At first, I didn't pay much attention to the Chinese guy who walked in the bar until he started to walk over. I watched as he pulled out a commando knife and plunged it into this bloke's chest, sat three people to my right. I remembered the sound of it entering his chest cavity, leaving the poor sod gasping for breath as I was splattered by a jet of blood. I half expected someone to shout, "Make way, I'm a doctor!" Instead, everyone ran for the door, so I followed.

Amsterdam had suddenly become a scary place, and I realised I could quite easily disappear or get killed, no questions asked. I had come here to do my rattle and had been hammered from day one; this wasn't working out.

As I ran out onto the street, it had kicked off, and everywhere there were people fighting. *This must be some sort of gang war, it's not my beef,* I thought.

I cut off down a narrow dimly lit alleyway in between two cafés and emerged outside a club where there was a queue for the place. Knowing the police were tied up around the corner, I did my best to blend in, to dip into a couple of pockets. Once I had some money, I was straight to Dam Square to see Pedro, the guy who I'd scored from at De vas. That night, I broke into an empty riverboat on the canal and got a peaceful night's sleep.

My health was really quite poor now, and the ulcers on my legs and ankles burned fiercely. My legs were badly swollen, and I was missing home and my mum and dad. I needed to get home. Next morning, I routed through my coat for my passport and ticket for the ferry. It wasn't there, "Bollocks," I said to myself. Things seemed to be going from bad to worse. I went to the British Consulate, where I used the phone. When Mum picked up the phone, I could feel a lump growing in my throat, and I fought back the tears. I knew if I let them flow, it would make her upset too, plus I'd get nothing sorted. I arranged for her to buy a ticket at her end and have the details faxed through. The woman in the Consulate squared everything for me to travel on some sort of pass, so now, all I had to do was survive long enough for my ticket, and I was away.

I'd never been so pleased as when I saw The White Cliffs of Dover.

I struggled down the road and walking was now exceptionally painful. As I walked in my local and put my pint down, I thought I'd take it easy and listen to the band for a while. A few mates were sat in the bay window behind me, deep in conversation. I just lit my rolly and looked up to see a broken bottle inches from my face. I heard him before I saw his face. "I'm no fucking scared of you," he said in broad Glaswegian accent. I was unable to make sense of what the guy was saying because I'm not someone who looks menacing or gets off on being threatening without reason. I looked him in the eyes and said, "What the fuck are you on about? I don't know you, I have never seen you before." He didn't respond to what I'd said. He just repeated his line, "I'm no fucking scared of you." I was more than concerned by the broken bottle that was coming ever nearer to my face. He had either mistaken me for someone else or was totally bonkers. I couldn't move with the broken bottle two inches from my face. In a split second, I grabbed his hair, pulled his face to mine, bit the end of his nose off and spat it on the carpet. The band had stopped playing, and this guy was screaming. I was surprised to see him run from the pub without his nose.

By this time Al, who'd been sat by the window, walked over to the nose, picked it up with a cocktail stick and placed it on the trophy shelf. I took the nose, put it inside a crisps bag (cheese and onion), so as not to touch it. By the time I went after this guy to reunite him with the nose, he was nowhere to be seen. Returning back to the pub, in case he showed up, the nose sat on the shelf next to a darts cup.

I did feel bad about the situation, but it was either him or me.

Chapter Seventeen

Back in prison, I started to face each day without drugs, which I found an exciting experience, and yet a frightening prospect, but I knew if I gave myself some time, my health would improve, so I clung onto this idea like a drowning man to a lifeboat. I didn't allow myself to look even a day ahead, those first few weeks; this was hard-core cold turkey. I only got the odd half an hour's sleep in about six weeks, which made sleep deprivation play weird tricks on my mind. I was convinced that the police had set up an observation in the cell next door. Witches talked to me through the bars on my windows, and as my temperature soared, I rambled on incoherently. My eyes streamed, and my nose ran constantly. I rolled on the floor trying to get some comfort from my aching bones, but muscle spasms made it impossible. I was exhausted yet knew I was fighting for my life and must carry on. I hadn't eaten for days, nothing stayed down.

I made my daily trip to the hatch for my aspirin water, then, after breakfast, onto the sick parade to see the doctor. I wasn't entirely sure which of these activities was the more pointless.

I went on a visit with my mum and dad, who couldn't quite believe their eyes at the wreck which sat before them.

I talked them through some of the last few weeks and where my head had been. My mum started to tell me they had put a claim for custody of Sarah, and soon there would be a court hearing. This gave me some hope, knowing that my daughter would soon be out of the children's home. Before they left, I reassured them I'd sit it out and not use any gear. We hugged, and I watched them walking out of the room.

My dad turned to me, smiled and said, "Keep your chin up, Phil, we love you." The small lump in my throat had now grown to a football as I choked back more tears.

I got back to my cell, banged the door shut, fell to my knees and prayed. I'd only prayed a couple of times in my life. Once, when I wanted bail, which didn't seem to work, and another occasion when my dog was ill. That didn't work either because he died. But this time was different because I wanted to cut a deal. I blocked my spy hole up for some privacy and said something like, "Dear God, I need some strength to get through this one. Please forgive me for the hurt and pain I've caused my family and others. *I'd like it if things were different between us. Please watch over my family and friends, Amen.*"

When I got up, I still felt rough, but there had certainly been some sort of shift in my thinking, as I felt more positive. I didn't want to become a religious person but was told by an old friend, who'd become clean, that in order to get my life sorted out, I needed a higher power. His words were, "Phil, you can't sort out a spiritual problem with a chemical solution." At the time, I thought he'd lost it, yet now it seemed to make sense. However, I was still in jail and had to deal with the reality of my situation, so I wasn't about to morph into some kind of saint.

I soon found myself stood in the dock at Preston Crown Court for sentencing.

I clearly remember the judge's words that day. "Phillip Grimes, you are a menace to society when in the commission of Class A drugs. I have heard your mitigation and read your reports; therefore, I am going to send you to prison for five years for the offence of robbery. And a further two years concurrently for false imprisonment. Take him down." I thought I'd done well getting seven years. It wasn't until a screw said to me, "You done well there, Grimesy Lad, pulling seven years," that I knew this sentence was a blessing in disguise for me.

I saw Mum and Dad in the visits underneath the court. They could see I was looking well physically, yet they were still upset it had come to this. I told them I loved them, and this was a new start; I meant it. The visit ended, and I had a brew, then I was led in cuffs to the sweatbox for the journey back to the nick.

Chapter Eighteen

There were no drug treatment programmes for anyone, as such, in 1991, other than aspirin water, the occasional Valium, and of course, being banged up. So I guess in that respect, some progress had been made. I knew it was up to me to seek out whatever help and support I could get. I asked my probation officer to get me a drugs counsellor, which in all fairness, he arranged. I attended the chapel and was given a lot of encouragement to keep pressing on. But even so, I knew this decision not to use again was one I would make on a daily basis.

My counsellor taught me how to feel more comfortable with my feelings and cope with the lunatic asylum that was now my head. Fears and insecurities about myself and prison life sometimes weighed me down. Yet I knew on another level, I had to keep walking forward to bring about change.

My emotions wouldn't kill me, opposed to the rubbish I used to pump into my system. Yet some days I felt like frustration, self-pity, low self-esteem and confidence were sent to torture me, specifically on this planet.

I did give my marriage a shot, but just a few months into my sentence, she was unfaithful to me, which set me back miles.

I didn't medicate myself, which seemed the most natural option at the time. However, once the screws had got wind of my letters, I was put on anti-depressants and suicide watch. After a few weeks of looking and feeling like a zombie, I stopped going for their pills.

I went on the education programme, thinking it's never too late to get an education and learned that my literacy skills were that of an eight-year-old. So I started to get the schooling I missed out on. At first, even the idea that I couldn't read and write properly was extremely uncomfortable, but I was quite determined and pretty stubborn. This made me a quick learner. I soon made progress.

I became a more accomplished reader, started reading books on how to improve self-confidence and other self-development books. I borrowed a book from one of my teachers on NLP (Neuro-Linguistic Programming), and this started to change the way I looked at things. It was all about improving your sensory experience so that when I read the back of it, my ears pricked up. Sensory deprivation was a really destructive part of prison for me, so one of the things I could now do was lessen the effects it was having on me. It also helped me to challenge some of my negative beliefs, which I held because my mental landscape contributed massively towards my dependency on drugs. For as long as I could remember, my creed had been *you might as well be hung for a sheep as a lamb*. This was a really destructive belief which had never done me any favours and contributed to my 'all or nothing' approach. My therapist constantly asked, "What purpose has this belief been serving until now?" I had always thought that beliefs were just written in stone and couldn't be changed. And I was stuck with the ones I'd developed, almost like a passive victim or prisoner to the way I'd been programmed; not true. I soon realised these beliefs were just ideas I'd held about myself and were not set in stone. When I started to look inside, I discovered a few that were harmful to me. It didn't matter how long I'd had some of these beliefs. In fact, some of the older, more ingrained beliefs, presented a greater challenge and had caused me the most harm. Some of my teachers' favourite catchphrases were: "You're stupid, Grimes! Trouble follows you wherever you go! You'll never make anything of yourself." Then, "Once a junkie, always a junkie." This belief kind of took away my power to even try to change my situation. I thought, *Oh well, might as well accept it and get on with the job*, and this idea had been rattling around my head for years. I'd even started to believe the 'menace to society' label that was spoken about me in court.

I was told to put an elastic band around my wrist and to ping it every time I caught myself saying this to myself. Then I'd counteracted this by saying, "I've made mistakes in the past, which can't be changed. But now I'm going to stay positive, be open-minded and re-write my future because I'm in control now, and not the drug." Now at first, it sounded a bit happy-clappy, but it worked because, little by little, it soaked into my unconscious mind, replacing the negative junk I'd been allowing my mind to focus on. I knew my old ways of thinking had caused me pain and disappointment and drove me to excess, now something had to change. I had to live in my own head, so why not make my head a better and easier place to spend time. I had plenty of great discussions with my therapist on this subject, and he introduced me to the think–feel–do cycle. Now I was putting a positive structure to my thoughts; it had the knock-on effect of making me feel better, which in turn made me feel more confident to cope without my chemical walking stick.

Over time, I started to become more objective and more flexible in my thinking. Most things had been cut and dried and very ridged. I had started my journey back to search for the real me that I'd lost. This recovery process was sometimes painful, and there were days where I was bouncing off the walls. Yet the peace of mind, self-fulfilment, and self-respect I'd gained drove me on because my life now had purpose to it. No more of the same old same old nonsense; each day was now different, and it didn't start by rattling. Even in jail, life was good because I was free inside myself. On previous sentences, my day would begin with either a powerful sense of anger, resentment, fear, or self-pity because these emotions ran the show. Most of my life, I had not felt good about myself, so I'd got hammered. I wanted to be someone else, somewhere else. I constantly escaped into the fantasy land of how fantastic the future would be if I had this, that, or the other. If I were not in fantasy land, I would revisit the past; at last, I had started to feel good about myself. This new thing I'd discovered now gave me the tools to re-arrange my memories, taking the power away from those memories that freaked me out. All these new ways I was discovering were making me stronger each day that passed.

I spoke with the chaplain, and he advised me to forgive Ann, my wife. So against my better judgement, I did. My parents visited me regularly, bringing Sarah, my daughter, up to see me. And after a couple of years, I was released to deal with a whole new monster. Staying clean on the outside.

Chapter Nineteen

I had been clean for nine years from leaving prison and had a certain amount of balance in my life, apart from in one area, my marriage.

I regretted not ending it when Ann had slept with this other guy whilst I was banged up, but I also knew it was in the past. The best thing to come out of my marriage with Ann was my daughter — Rae. She was the glue that held us together for a long time; otherwise, I would have left earlier. Rae was full of life; a beautiful little girl who gave me a purpose to keep going. She was a right character, cheeky, funny, and full of energy.

I had developed leg ulcers on my ankles because of injecting into my groin and was finding the pain almost unbearable.

I had gone a couple of months with only an hour or two's sleep each night. My ankles were on fire with pain, and there was no escape from it, and things were now coming to a head. I wasn't eating properly or thinking straight. Pain dominated my every waking moment. I didn't want to be considered a failure or to let others down, including myself. My need for pain relief was now greater than my need for the recovery or anything else, come to think of it. I remember saying to myself, *Fuck it, I'm going to see the doctor*. I'd got past even caring as I felt like I had rats constantly eating away at the flesh around my ankles; I had to switch it off.

As I sat in front of the doctor with tears running down my face, I realised I couldn't go on like this anymore. I showed him my wounds and hoped he could do something. "Mr Grimes, how come you have let yourself get into this kind of mess?" he said. He wrote me a script for a Morphine Sulphate mixture, which I knew would kill the pain. And if it didn't, I'd be so off my head, I wouldn't be capable of thinking too hard about it. He made a referral to a specialist and had a nurse put dressings on for me.

I took the Morphine as prescribed for the first couple of months. I didn't need extra; as my tolerance to opiates was low, it blew my head off. I continued to work at the homeless shelter and was able to do my job pain-free. Only I was totally off my face, and of course, luckily no one had sussed me out.

A few months had raced by; Ann and I argued almost continually about Morphine. I would say with venom, "It's me that's in pain, and unless you can come to me with an alternative, leave me alone." She didn't, and so I carried on.

When my ulcers had improved, and it was time to come off the Morphine, this was where I struggled. It was almost like a child and an adult having a tug of war over a comfort blanket. Me on one end, my doctor on the other. He won but not without a fight. I lied through my teeth and used all my best manipulation tactics. The doctor didn't seem to give a toss that I was now dependant on the Morphine that he'd given me and refused to give me any more. I told him to "Fuck off!" and slammed the door behind me. I knew I needed some more; otherwise, I would rattle. I went to the cash machine, then scored a couple of bags.

Before long, I was sitting in this smelly, dirty flat with a belt around my foot trying to find a vein. The windows were that filthy, I couldn't see who was banging on it, and I didn't care either. It was an address which I guess would have been watched carefully by the police, as there had been a couple of drug deaths there.

All sorts of heads just used the place for a hit or to crash. There were people smashed out of their heads all over the joint, yet I never worked out whose flat it actually was. I felt both regret and relief when blood flooded into my works, which by the time the gear hit me, was replaced by a warm inner glow, the type which feels like a small piece of heaven. I felt like those nine years of clean time were a figment of my imagination. What had I done? What was happening to me?

But it got worse: the circus came to town. At first, I was an observer of this circus that was crack cocaine. I had used crack on the odd occasion, which immediately plugged me into a world of madness and insanity, so I had done my best to consciously avoid it. Crack reconnected me with the psychosis I had been through towards the end of my amphetamine use. I thought the only real purpose of cocaine was to sling it in the barrel as a snowball, which would then enable me to use more opiates and ride it out. I found the whole experience of smoking crack a bit like coming down stairs on Christmas morning to see lots of presents round the tree, only to open them to find them empty — disappointing.

Yes, crack was intense and, yes, it was far better than snorting coke, but to me it was a pointless experience that rendered me unproductive and paranoid. As a drug, it was a bit like someone dragging their fingernails down a blackboard. However, once I had dipped my toe in and had enough of a taste, I then entered the world of the paranoid. I found myself driven by a force I didn't really understand — to score this stuff, then smoke it, and neither of which I particularly enjoyed.

I now ordered a rock with my gear, and felt like I had to indulge this mental obsession just to feel even half human. I'd smoke a rock to feel the euphoria of the hit — then get totally depressed. The promise and illusion of crack gave me something more than I already had, kept me on the endless search for more. After a few years of this circus, I started to really hate the stuff. I hated what this drug had turned me into, and wanted out.

I spent large periods of my time either ducking and diving to get money to buy it, scoring it off the dodgy fuckers who sell it, and chicken-picking my way around many a carpet, convinced I had dropped a bit once I'd had a pipe. Somehow I always managed to trick myself into believing there was some on the floor, or, once I had got bored with that one, then *"someone was trying to rip me off."* A more empty existence I cannot imagine, but this is the mental game of someone who has been bitten by the crack monster, played out on an endless loop.

I went to meet a dealer one day and peddled about 3 miles on an old mountain bike in the pissing-down rain. It was freezing. En route, a bus passed me on the road and forced me into the curb. This sent me over the handlebars, grazing my face and smashing up my hand. I finally got there, and the dealer didn't show. I was bursting for a piss, my hand was throbbing, and I'd lost my money along the way — long live Groundhog Day! I returned home empty-handed, and pissed off about the whole thing. I was now tired and needed the chance to get my shit together and if that was to happen I would snatch someone's hand off to get it. Another phone call later and I had it delivered. After a few more days of paranoid chicken-picking and insanity, I got some decent gear and sacked it off. That was the end of my affair with crack.

A week had passed since I left home to go for my doctor's appointment, and I knew I must go home and face the music. I cleaned the mirror with a blood-stained tissue which I'd used to wipe my groin. I spat at the mirror, angrily, thinking, *Who lives like this?* And as I looked at my reflection, I answered my own question. *You do, Phil.* I was starting to look gaunt in the face. I'd not eaten much, and my junkie face was back. I didn't like what I was looking at and wondered what sort of story I could come up with to tell Ann. She wasn't daft; she'd been there herself. Might as well tell her the truth. It was obvious, wasn't it?

As the front door opened, the screaming began. *"Where the fuck have you been?"* And after that, it was all one noise. I learned years before how to switch off when I didn't want to hear the truth, and this was a massive part of my problem, selective hearing. I had my own way of filtering out what had been said to me, especially if I didn't like it or it hurt. I distorted painful comments and made them acceptable for me to live with by attaching my own meaning and interpretation. "Oh well, everyone uses some sort of crutch." Do they, everyone?

Eventually, after much argument, I agreed to go into a Christian community for drug addiction in the Midlands. Really, only because I felt that my options were limited. I wasn't registered at the CDT anymore, and even if I was, it took months for the funding to be secured. I'd had friends who had died whilst they were left dangled on a waiting list for detox or rehab. I knew from experience; I had to act quickly before I disappeared back into heroin and was swallowed whole. I could use a bad situation for a good purpose, as I had done in prison all those years ago. My manager offered to keep my job open, so off I went.

This Christian community place reminded me of some sort of sci-fi cult; like a hippy commune. The minute I walked through the door, they took my roll-ups off me, and I was told I was now a non-smoker. All my possessions were taken which I'd expected. I was rattling by now and told, "There's no medication given here. When you're feeling bad enough, one of the brothers will pray for you." This was too full on for me. I believe in God, yet, I also believe that everyone deserves to be shown unconditional love, compassion, understanding, and respect.

I soon came to understand that these people wanted control over my mind, so I decided to do my turkey and leave. They wanted me to work restoring furniture, whilst listening to Christian worship music. We were not allowed to listen to any other music. This furniture was then sold in outlets owned by the community, and it was managed by those who had eventually yielded to this whole trip. There was absolutely no watching TV, lest we were corrupted by the big, bad world. Besides anything else, I could have killed for a cigarette and could have done without attending chapel every morning, whilst feeling strung out. This place was more like a cult than anything else. Financially, the community was self-sufficient, so they didn't rely on government funding. This was how they wanted it, so they didn't have to compromise their biblical position. In other words, they were not regulated by anyone so they could do what they wanted. And they did! Not my understanding of rehab. The Bible was used like a tommy gun to instil guilt and shame, so after six weeks, once I was feeling better, I split. However much I disagreed with their wacky ideas about the demons of addiction dwelling in the hearts of addicts, there were some sound lads in that place who were like myself and were vulnerable yet had bought into the whole philosophy. One guy had been drug-free for two years yet was told he wasn't ready to even travel the fifty yards down the lane to the post box.

    I left clean again and ready to get on with life. I was glad to get back to work. I loved working with the kids in the homeless project; we had plenty of common ground, more than they would ever know. It was obvious to me that one of their biggest needs was to be listened to and feel understood. So I made sure I had time to sit with them, so they could talk and I could listen.

I had started to attend the local college to study criminology. I thought as it was a subject where I'd had some hands-on practical experience, I might enjoy a chance of learning what the experts had to say on the matter, which I found really interesting. Something else of great interest to me was the lady who I was sat next to.

She was a petite blonde, with blue eyes, and she was stunning. We talked at breaks in the canteen, and I realised we had loads in common; she was really warm and kind with a great sense of humour.

Her name was Susy, and we shared lots of interests. Susy started working at the same hostel as me, so we got even more opportunities to chat.

I had developed powerful feelings for Susy, so now I decided to let her know how I felt. I called in at the hostel one evening to tell her. I took a deep breath and walked into the smoky staff room, asked her to sit down and found myself telling her how I felt. Once the initial shock wore off, Susy told me. She told me to go home to my wife and sort my marriage out, but I had decided to leave my wife a long time before yet had waited for the right time. Then I realised there would never be one. My main concern was for Rae, but I knew it was for the best that I leave. I would speak with Rae once I was out of the house, as she was too young to understand. When I stood at the front door, I said goodbye to Charlotte, my lurcher, and left the house for the last time. This was something I'd thought long and hard about. A sense of relief swept over me when I put my cases in the back of the car and drove to my sister's place.

It was during one of Rae's visits to my sister's house that I felt stabbing pains in my legs. I was playing cards with Rae when I first noticed the burning pain return. All sorts of nonsense went through my mind. Was my body shutting down? After the madness in my head subsided, I realised it was the consequences of my drug taking. "Just my fucking luck," I said as self-pity set in. I wasn't going to sit around in agony this time; I was straight to the doctors. He gave me a script of DF'S and Nitrazepam, then referred me to the tissue viability nurse to do my dressings.

I had started seeing Susy, which made me feel alive. She knew how to make me laugh. I felt complete when I was with her. We would spend hours and hours just talking. Susy was the first woman I'd been out with that had never been into drugs, and I liked that. She was fresh, exciting, full of life, and beautiful. I just knew for certain that I wanted to be with her for the rest of my life. After a few months of us being together, I asked her to marry me, and although I had no ring to give her, she said yes. Later, I moved in with Susy, and we planned to get married. Susy didn't want a big affair or do, she wasn't into the 'white wedding' thing and suggested the registry office. The date was booked, just a few weeks away. I was trying to keep a grip on my drug use daily and hated lying to Susy. I had so much respect for her and didn't want married life starting out this way. I was glad though that she didn't know anything about how addicts behave, and I could manipulate situations so I could nip off and buy drugs. Our wedding day arrived, and I was so happy. It was one of the best days of my life; I was marrying my best friend and the woman of my dreams.

With our two closest friends, we tied the knot, and it was a lovely day. A two-day honeymoon and we were back home, the reality of my drug use and pain from my ulcers were really getting to me. Susy was cottoning on to my chaotic comings and goings, and after a few months, she told me to move out and go and sort my life out. Susy was a woman who had order in her life, always. She had a routine for her and the kids and wouldn't let anything get in that way. I moved into a flat a couple of miles away. Susy would come around occasionally to see me, looking at me pitifully and begging me to get help for my drug use. My leg ulcers were still killing me, but my drug habit was out of control again. Our first wedding anniversary was coming up, and I couldn't believe I had made such a mess of things; Susy was the love of my life, and she was slipping away from me. One evening, I went to a friend's house to score. There was a young woman there, very attractive, slim. She was into cocaine. We got on well enough — her, off her head on coke, me on gear, and we spent the night together. I moved in with her the next day. A couple of days later (not remembering), it was my first wedding anniversary to Susy. I popped around to my mum's with Cheryl in the car, to introduce her to my parents. As I pulled up to my mum's, Susy was just getting into her car; she had an anniversary card in her hand that she was leaving at my mum's. Cheryl was in the car with me, and at this point, the shit hit the fan, big time (Susy didn't know about Cheryl until now).

Susy asked who Cheryl was. I lied, but Susy is far from stupid and flipped. She told me the marriage was over, and I was gutted. What the hell was I doing? I was full on back into the gear, and my marriage to Susy was now over. I got back in my car and drove off with Cheryl. A few days later at my mum's house, a big brown envelope was waiting for me. Divorce proceedings from Susy. I was devastated, gutted as I read the words from Susy's solicitor. I just wanted her back; I wanted to spend the rest of my life with her, and once again I had fucked up big time.

The Journey Back

I desperately wanted to save my marriage to Susy. I had put her through hell, and I loved her, but with my behaviour she was getting to the end. I would go and see my drug worker who on every appointment appeared surprised I was still alive; to look at me, you wouldn't have given me a cat in hell's chance of changing my life. I had lost a lot of weight, and I had hepatitis C. I'd got to the point where I had to just do it and get some recovery and embrace it or shut up and quietly embrace the inevitable. I really wanted this more than anything — for myself and knew I would have to put the same energy and commitment that I put into my addiction into getting well. I would have walked over broken glass in my bare feet to get my drugs, so now I had to re-channel that same energy and commitment for something positive. I got the chance to go to rehab; the only place on offer to me was Pierpoint House which if I am honest would not have been my first choice, but I thought, *It is what it is, go and make the most of it*, as I was grateful of the opportunity to change my life. After eight weeks, I left, and part of me was excited about what my life would now hold, yet another part of me was nervous. I knew this was the real deal now, and I was determined to give it my best shot. Susy stood by me through rehab, and our marriage became stronger than ever.

I knew I would have to find a different path for my recovery other than the prescribed recovery models, as I didn't feel they were a good fit for me. I had enjoyed going to the fellowships because I met some great people there and being around like-minded people made me believe it was possible to change. It didn't take me long to work out that probably a more eclectic approach to my recovery would be more beneficial to me. I had always been cautious about a one-size-fits-all approach to anything in life and the same too with recovery. I now know it's horses for courses, and what might be right for one might not work not the next person. I took some CBT, some Buddhism, some NLP and as much positive psychology as I could get, and applied that to my life. I knew it would move me forwards. I also knew the importance of staying connected with like-minded people as a support network. I also looked up a good coach to direct me.

I remembered reading an NLP book which discussed modelling, so I looked at the lives of people who'd overcome adversity to see what lessons there were to be learned and also how I could apply them to my life. I spent many months reading about how to change thoughts, which to me was refreshing. I had heard a lot about "you need to change your behaviour," but I always wondered how to do that. All I knew was that a lot of my thinking was toxic, and I'd had a bad attitude for far too long. From the learning I had done (Susy and I went on an NLP course), things started to fall into place.

So now I had a clue where to focus my attention.

After six months of being home, I wanted to find some work. I first started working in a supported housing unit for people with learning difficulties, which I absolutely loved. Then came an opportunity to work as a community outreach adviser working with long-term unemployed people targeting those who had drug or alcohol problems, mental health issues, and homelessness, as well as offenders. I really enjoyed this job and got to meet some amazing people. I bounced out of bed in the morning to get there. My colleague Darren was a brilliant laugh and had me in stitches every day. I told him little bits about my past life, and he was surprised, but never judged me negatively for it. When we took the work vehicle out to the estates, our nicknames were Max and Paddy. We had such a laugh, but we got the work done. Some of the clients that we would talk to were living my old life, wanting to get a break to sort themselves out, so we would point them in the direction of the drug and alcohol services in town. I would be going to the areas where I once would have scored. Did it trigger me? No, but it brought up memories which I used to motivate me to stay clean, and get the job in hand done.

My role involved going to homeless hostels, psychiatric hospitals, and drug and alcohol treatment services, and delivering training to prepare them for the world of employment. I did that role for a number of years, which helped me grow as a person because I was continually finding myself out of my comfort zone and being stretched in all directions; however, it was time for a move.

I got a job working at the drug/alcohol services in Blackpool. This was a great job too where I met some great people, and my time was split between working on the community rehab or in the detox house. My co-workers were a good bunch. I started on day-one with another guy called Barry, who I hit it off with straight away. I worked alongside Barry in setting up the detox house. He was in recovery himself, knowledgeable and had an endless stream of very funny stories about his life that kept me laughing. It was an organisation that knew how to treat people with respect — people who had drug and alcohol problems, from the most chaotic and difficult to those who were stable and in recovery. I had some great teachers, and I soaked up as much as I could. The respect came from the management down; the manager and head of service there were brilliant. I met people who will be friends for life.

I was asked to visit a private rehab by a friend of mine who worked there. It had recently opened, and I was asked to have a look around it to see what I thought of it. I wasn't told it was a job interview, and as it turned out, the owners found my past experience and skills exactly what they were looking for. I was offered the job there and then. I facilitated groups, did one-to-one coaching with clients, and enjoyed my work. I got the chance to join up with a very experienced psychotherapist in groups and loved every minute of it, and I witnessed people making life-changing decisions about their futures. I suppose the highlight for me was working with Rick. Rick was a doctor who was in recovery who ran workshops on the neuroscience of addiction. He would tell stories of his addiction to heroin and alcohol, and then describe what was going on in our body at a physical and neurological level, which made it all relevant and real. This place was an eye-opener for me as previously I'd worked with the homeless or people who were using drugs at a street level. Here, the clients were mostly professionals and various other types of business executives/owners. Lovely people. It struck me very early on in the job that the only difference with this client group was that having money meant getting into rehab quicker.

I decided to further my career and do some more training, so I first did my training and certification as a life coach and from there went on to train as a professionally certified recovery coach. I had previously got a Master Practitioner certification in NLP, so my recent training complemented this. I had started taking on more private clients on my days off and began to build up a client practice of my own.

I have always been a big fan of CPD (Continuing Personal Development); we tend to only use this in our professional lives, but I really think that we should take a yearly CPD in our personal lives as well. I immerse myself in self-development books and courses and don't tire of trying to find better ways to live a balanced, peaceful, and stress-free life. I haven't just sat back in my recovery and taken it for granted or got complacent. I live my life, but I also look after myself — and with Susy being a Nutritional Therapist, I eat well. I finished my treatment for Hep C last year, which was a huge relief, so I am now Hep C-free!

Life was (and is) good again. I had some relationship-building to do with my daughters, who were hoping they would finally get their dad back. Rae has a career in hairdressing, and is a pleasure to be around. We have a great laugh when we're together and get on well. My relationship with her mother is non-existent now Rae's grown up. However, it's civil and polite if we meet.

Sarah, is a fabulous mother of three — my grandchildren who I adore. They are an absolute credit to her; lovely, polite, well-mannered young children, who have me in hysterics with some of the things they do and say. I'm very proud of Sarah; she is quiet and considered in her approach to life like me, but nobody's fool. We have a great relationship now, and are very similar in our personalities. I haven't seen Sarah's mum for many years.

My mum is now eighty-three years old, and quite sprightly for her age. The matriarch of the family, my mum has been through the worst with me, but always stuck by me. I love her very much.

I used to feel that there was always somewhere else to be other than here in this moment. I have learned so much from my many teachers through life. Happiness is always an inside job.

NOT THE END

CPSIA information can be obtained
at www.ICGtesting.com
Printed in the USA
LVHW032345040222
710176LV00003B/168

9 781999 869007